SPICE IS RIGHT

EASY
INDIAN COOKING
FOR TODAY

Monica Bhide

Callawind
Publications Inc.

The Spice Is Right: Easy Indian Cooking for Today

Copyright © 2001 by Monica Bhide

CATALOGUING IN PUBLICATION DATA

Bhide, Monica, 1969–

The spice is right : easy Indian cooking for today

Includes index.

ISBN 1-896511-17-1

1. Cookery, Indic. 2. Quick and easy cookery. 3. Menus.
I. Title.

TX724.5.I4B55 2001   641.5954   C2001-901707-3

Copy editing by Shaun Oakey. Design by Marcy Claman. Indexing by Christine Jacobs.
Cover photo of Indian spice, raked in abstract design © Digital Vision.

10 9 8 7 6 5 4 3 2 1

Printed in Canada.

All product/brand names are trademarks or registered trademarks of their respective trademark holders.

Callawind Publications Inc.

3539 St. Charles Boulevard, Suite 179, Kirkland, Quebec, Canada H9H 3C4
2083 Hempstead Turnpike, PMB 355, East Meadow, New York, USA 11554-1711
E-mail: info@callawind.com   http://www.callawind.com

FOR NIRMALA:
YOU ARE MY TRUE TREASURE

acknowledgments

I would like to thank the following people for their support, encouragement, and advice in writing this book. My grandmothers influenced my cooking a great deal, and though they are not around to see this book , I know in my heart that they are watching.

- ❋ The late Mrs. Kaushalya Saigal, my grandmother
- ❋ The late Mrs. Savitri Malik, my grandmother
- ❋ Dina and Sneh Saigal, my parents
- ❋ BM and Shashi Bhide, my in-laws
- ❋ Arti and Sumir Bahl, my sister and brother-in-law
- ❋ Shree and Smita Gondhalekar
- ❋ Kedar and Vrinda Deval
- ❋ Meena Mehra
- ❋ Ankur and Anubha Rohatgi
- ❋ Nina Rohatgi
- ❋ Dimple Agarwal, Roopa Wardekar, Karen Gazzara, Kedar Pandit, Mike and Patti Corrigan, and Biren and Sujata Kapoor for their marketing help

- ❋ My friends, Sandy Turba, Makrand and Meghana Bhave, Anil Nair, Vivek Jog, and Mani and Nischint Kumar for all their encouragement and support
- ❋ S. Malik
- ❋ Sunita Godbole
- ❋ My numerous recipe testers/advisors/tasters from Ernst & Young and Knowledge Impact
- ❋ Sr. Fransisca
- ❋ Shilpa Thakur, senior nutritionist
- ❋ Dr. Suresh Chandra
- ❋ Shaun Oakey for his amazing editing skills

This book would not have been made possible without my publisher, Marcy Claman. I would finally like to thank my wonderful husband, Sameer, whose love and support have made this a reality for me today. Last but not least, I would like to thank my toddler, Jai . . . his running around the house with my manuscript shouting "Mama's book, Mama's book" was a true inspiration!

contents

NECESSITY IS THE MOTHER OF INVENTION, or, in my case, documentation! Almost a decade ago, when I moved to the United States, I would find myself constantly calling home to India and Bahrain to get recipes from my mom or my aunt or my cousins. The phone bills were exorbitant, a lot higher than the ingredients for the recipes! I started a journal and began writing down my favorite recipes. So began a wonderful journey. And a much less expensive one.

In addition to Mom's familiar cooking, I was also eager to try new recipes. Sometimes it was wonderful, other times it was intimidating, particularly when the recipes called for ingredients that I had never heard of, much less seen in stores. (Try looking for banana leaves in Cleveland in January.) I tried to refashion the recipes without the exotic ingredients. I had one goal: the recipe had to be simple to make, delicious to eat, and easy on the weight and the wallet. My little journal grew into a binder, then into a wedding present for my sister, Arti, and now I present it to you. My life's work is in this book. Here is my collection of Indian soul food, comfort food that is delicious and nutritious.

Here's what I have learnt as a home chef: teaspoons of spices are never too much, tablespoons of oil are just enough, and a little bit of imagination goes a long way! Use these recipes as a starting point: play with the amounts and kinds of spices, a pinch here and a pinch there, until you have it just the way you want it. After all, that is the difference between a cook and a chef! Same goes with the timing provided in each recipe. Yours may vary a little because of the cut of meat or the heat of your oven. There is no right or wrong here — just great meals waiting to happen.

The book is laid out in menus. Each menu has drinks, appetizers, entrées, side dishes, and desserts. In Indian homes you rarely find a person eating one dish. Usually a combination of dishes are served, and people enjoy small portions of each. Most of the menus in this book are fairly elaborate, intentionally. I wanted to provide you with a wide range of dishes that you could choose from. For the busy cook, I have included an express menu in each chapter. Pick and choose from the menu, try a few at a time, and discover what you like.

Each menu concludes with a section on what to do with leftovers. I hate wasting food, but I also found eating plain leftovers boring. So I decided to see what I could "cook up" with the leftovers. There were some experiments that I should have left alone (!), but many lend themselves well to the metamorphosis.

introduction

My recipes do not require involved cooking techniques. I have tried to provide a variation for each recipe, along with helpful cooking or serving tips or information about particular ingredients.

As well, I have included Web Bites, links to various wonderful informational sites on the Internet. In addition there are links to on-line grocery stores where you can buy Indian ingredients if you can't find them in your stores.

There are a couple of informational sections in the book. The Spice Sack describes what is in a typical Indian pantry. There is a description of basic cooking techniques used in this book and also a short list of Indian grocery stores.

I worked with Shilpa Thakur, a senior nutritionist at Escort Hospital and Research Center Limited in Faridabad, North Delhi, to provide a nutritional analysis for each recipe. A disclaimer is due here: This is not your usual healthy cookbook where every single recipe has less than a gram of fat. Although I have tried to keep the recipes as healthy as possible, I have included some that are higher in fat content. If you are concerned about your fat intake, my advice to you is try such recipes in limited portions. There is more to some dishes than their fat content. There is tradition and memories. Don't deprive yourself, just limit the portions.

The nutritional analysis takes into account only the main ingredients in each recipe, not any garnishes or optional ingredients. Since salt is to taste, it was excluded from the analysis. Any quantity less than 0.5 grams is listed as "trace." Regular vegetable oil (canola oil) is used throughout.

Recipes that use hot ingredients have a heat indicator:
*   Mild (Translation: What is this doing in a spicy cookbook?)
**   Medium (Translation: I can eat this and my stomach will still love me.)
***   Hot (Translation: I can eat this and my stomach might love me.)
**** Author refuses to take any responsibility for this category.

Sometimes cookbooks are hard to follow. A pregnant friend once called me and told me this story. Since she was nine months along, her husband decided to cook dinner for her one night. So he got out his Indian cookbook and proceeded. My friend, who was upstairs, heard a racket in the kitchen and went down to see what was going on. There he was waving frantically over a plate of potatoes. "What are you doing, honey?" she asked. His reply: "Well, the book says, slice the potatoes and fan them." Good thing they did not ask him to whip the cream! If you have a question about a recipe, or need help finding an ingredient, visit my Web site at http://www.spiceisright.net or drop me a line at author@spiceisright.net. I will do my best to respond quickly.

What you see here is a collection of memories. I believe that everything you eat evokes a memory of something. Many of these dishes remind me of Sunday mornings with my mother, when I was learning to cook. The grilled recipes are my father's treasures. Some remind me of disasters that my husband, Sameer, had to put up with before I got it right, and some remind me of warm evenings with friends in front of a toasty roaring fireplace. Go ahead, try a few recipes, and make your own memories.

a few words on nutritional guidelines

. . . .

"Never eat what you cannot lift" — Miss Piggy

Indian cuisine is traditionally a rich cuisine, with lots of ghee (clarified butter), coconut milk, full-fat paneer, etc. I have tried to select recipes that still provide the richness but not the high saturated fats. The following guidelines have been used in this book:

※ Recipes have been modified for grilling or baking wherever possible to avoid deep-frying

※ In recipes where deep-frying is unavoidable, serving sizes have been reduced

※ Low-fat substitutes have been used (for example: using tofu instead of high-fat cottage cheese and low-fat coconut milk instead of the regular high-fat variety)

※ I have tried to replace fats without losing taste by using innovative herb and spice mixtures instead of oil and butter, including marinating ingredients in herbs and spices

※ Within each menu, if one dish is unavoidably calorie-heavy, the other recipes are purposely calorie-light (except the Turkey Day menu)

※ The leftover suggestions encourage you to whip up wholesome additional dishes instead of ordering in or taking out fast food

IN INDIA, THERE REALLY IS NO SUCH THING AS CURRY POWDER; spices are sold separately, and people make their own blends. "Curry" is a Western term invented to describe any spicy gravy. I have been hard pressed to find an Indian equivalent. Some famous Indian cooks, such as Camellia Panjabi, note that the word simply means "gravy." In 1780 the first commercial curry powder appeared in Great Britain, and there has been no looking back.

However, for all of you who think that Indian food is all about curry, get ready for an adventure. The contrasts and flavors of Indian cuisine are fascinating. Most of the food is tailored to locally grown crops and spices, yet the food is as varied as the landscape, from the mountaintops of the Himalayas to the Indian Ocean to the luscious green fields of the State of Punjab to the tropical beaches of Kerala. The cuisine has also been greatly influenced by the multitude of religions in India. In India there are cookbooks for orthodox Jains, or Brahmins, who will not eat any root vegetables, and for Hindus, who will not eat beef. The country has 900 million people, who speak more than 16 languages in 200 dialects, and a varied cuisine to match.

To learn about Indian history, study the cuisine. Vinegar will talk of the Portuguese; rice dishes laden with dried fruit speak of the Moguls; tea will whisper about the Queen; and pistachios and coffee will tell stories of the Arab traders. Cookbook writer Madhur Jaffrey said it best: "No foreign food was discarded. It was just made Indian."

My native Delhi in North India has one characteristic that I love: people love to eat and drink and be merry. The rich and spicy food of Delhi has been influenced by the Mogul Empire. The generous nature of Delhi-ites is legendary. They love to entertain and sub-scribe to the old Indian philosophy of "athithi devo bhava," which means that a guest is the form of God and should be treated as such. You will be fed and fed and fed some more! I think my grandmother summed it up the best. When I was learning to cook, she always said to me: "Cook like you are expecting company." I abide by it; my husband says there is always enough food to feed an army at our house!

The folks in the South are simpler. Their staple is simple rice and lentil preparations, very different from the rich sauces of the North. Fish and other seafood is popular, compared with chicken and lamb in the North. South Indian side dishes, chutneys, and pickles are truly scrumptious. In fact, I consider them the crowning glory of South Indian food. Coconuts are abundant in the coastal climate, and they are used generously in the region's cuisine. One state in the South, Andhra Pradesh, is known for its nonvegetarian and rice dishes influenced greatly by the Nizams, the ruling Moslem emperors of the 1500s.

The cuisine of Eastern India revolves around freshwater seafood. Coconut, mustard seeds, and mustard oil are used abundantly in this cuisine. And the desserts are to die for.

My husband, Sameer, hails from Bombay in Western India. The locals in the western states of Maharastra and Gujarat are predominantly vegetarians. Their cuisine is lighter and often uses lentils and rice. Sugar-flavored dishes are greatly favored. The most interesting cuisine of this region, I think, comes from Goa. I love Goan food so much that the first menu in this book is dedicated to it. Goa was ruled by the Portuguese, and its cuisine reflects the strong use of spices and vinegar.

In India, most food is cooked in ghee, a close cousin to clarified butter. Various books call it the sinful butter, since it is high in saturated fat. It is — this one I cannot defend! But like everything in life, try it at least once. A tablespoon is all that is needed to give your dishes a wonderful nutty authentic Indian flavor. You can use ghee for tempering, or tadka, in any of the recipes in this book. In the South and Western India, coconut oil and mustard oil are also frequently used as the cooking fat.

The manner in which food is eaten in India is quite different from in the Western world. You eat with your hands, not with forks and knifes. This is hard for many Westerners to understand, but I will tell you a secret: it tastes better with your hands. Try it! It will go against that voice in your head that says, "Eat with your fork, son/daughter." But try it — it makes Indian food that much more wonderful.

So what is common to the cuisine in this land of diversity? You guessed it: spices. The same spices in different textures and forms and in different quantities and combinations is what unifies the nation's cuisine.

the spice sack

Here are descriptions of the herbs, spices, and lentils used in this book. If you wish to know more, here is a very informative site devoted to spices: http://www.menumagazine.co.uk/azfood.htm

Almonds (badam): Almonds were introduced into Indian cooking by the Persians. They are available whole, skinned (blanched), slivered, and ground, and impart a milky richness to curries and other dishes. They are considered a great delicacy in India.

Asafetida (hing): This is a resin with a bitter taste and a strong odor. The strong smell disappears as the resin cooks. Adding asafetida to lentils while they cook dissipates gas from them and makes them easier to digest. Add just a pinch to get the powerful flavor.

Basmati rice: This long-grain rice has a distinctive nutty flavor and a wonderful fragrance when cooked. The word "basmati" means "the Queen of Fragrance." Basmati rice is aged to intensify its flavor. The older the rice, the better it tastes.

Bay leaves (tej patta): These large dried leaves of the bay laurel tree are one of the oldest herbs used in cookery. They are not a substitute for curry leaves.

Black-eyed peas (lobiya): These white kidney-shaped beans with a black "eye" are available dried and canned.

Cardamom: This wonderfully aromatic spice is sold whole or ground. For true flavor, buy the pods and grind the seeds just before using them.

Carom seeds or bishops weed (ajwain seeds): These small seeds have a pungent smell and resemble cumin seeds. They have strong digestive properties.

Chappati flour (atta): This is a type of whole meal (whole-wheat flour) available from Asian stores and is used to make chappatis and other Indian breads.

Chickpeas (chole): This nutty pulse is used widely in Indian dishes. Chickpea flour, or besan, is made from chickpeas and is used in batters or to thicken curries.

Chiles, dried whole red (saboot lal mirch): These hot peppers are extremely fiery and should be used with caution. Dried chiles can be used whole or coarsely crushed. The smaller ones are hotter in taste. Remove the seeds to tone down the heat.

Chiles, fresh green (hari mirch): Green chiles are indispensable to Indian cuisine. They are very rich in vitamins A and C.

Cinnamon (dal chini): Cassia bark is a spice similar to true cinnamon. Do not substitute ground cinnamon for cinnamon sticks. Cassia is a much stronger spice than the real cinnamon.

Cloves (laung): This spice is used to flavor many sweet and savory dishes and is usually added whole. It is native to Indonesia. Cloves are actually dried flower buds of an evergreen tree native to Southeast Asia. Chewing a clove is an age-old remedy for a toothache.

Coconut: Used to flavor both sweet and savory dishes, fresh coconut is now frequently available in supermarkets. Most Indian stores — and many supermarkets — carry dried coconut as well.

Coriander, fresh (hara dhaniya): This beautifully fragrant herb is used both in cooking and sprinkled over dishes as an attractive garnish. It's also known as cilantro and Chinese parsley. Do not substitute dried coriander for fresh coriander.

Coriander, seeds and ground (dhaniya): This aromatic spice has a pungent, slightly lemony flavor. The seeds are used widely, either coarsely ground or in powdered form, in meat, fish, and poultry dishes. Coriander is perhaps the most widely used spice in Indian cooking.

Cumin seeds (jeera): Cumin seeds are dark and are used to flavor curries and rice. They are used whole or ground. Dry roasting cumin seeds brings out their wonderful aroma and flavor.

Curry leaves (kari patta): Similar in appearance to bay leaves, curry leaves give food a wonderful aroma and savory flavor. They are an important herb in South Indian cooking. Fresh leaves freeze well. Curry powder has no connection to curry leaves and is not a substitute.

Fennel seeds (saunf): Very similar in appearance to cumin seeds, fennel seeds have a delicate licorice flavor and add a zesty note to curries. They are often served at the end of a meal as a digestive aid.

Fenugreek seeds (methi): These flat seeds are extremely pungent and slightly bitter. They are used frequently in South Indian cooking and in the preparation of pickles. Dried fenugreek leaves (kasoori methi) are often added to dishes to give them a wonderful fragrance and taste.

Garam masala: This mixture of strong and aromatic spices is used to add zest and fragrance to many dishes. There is no set recipe for the blend, and many families have their own recipe. I have included my version on page 18.

Mango powder (amchoor): Made from dried unripe mangoes, this powder has a sour taste. If it is not available, use lemon juice as a substitute.

Masoor dal: These split red lentils are actually orange in color and turn a pale yellow when cooked. Masoor provides a nutty flavor when cooked. Cooked masoor dal has the consistency of porridge.

Moong (or mung) dal: These teardrop-shaped split yellow lentils are easy to cook and digest. They become very creamy when cooked.

Mustard seeds, black: Round in shape and sharp in flavor, black mustard seeds are used for flavoring curries and pickles.

Paneer: Indian homemade cottage cheese. See my recipe on page 18.

Peppercorns: Black peppercorns are sometimes used whole with other whole spices, such as cloves, cardamom pods, and bay leaves, to flavor curries.

Pomegranate seeds (anardana): These are taken from fresh pomegranate and are used as is or added to salads and chaats.

Red chile powder (lal mirch): This fiery ground spice should be used with caution. The heat can vary from brand to brand. On a trip to India a couple of years ago, I counted 18 types of chile powders at a local grocer.

Saffron: This is the world's most expensive spice. Dried threads are crushed and infused in milk before they are used. Store in the refrigerator, as this spice loses its fragrance quickly.

Sesame seeds: These seeds have a slightly nutty taste.

Star anise: Star anise is a star-shaped licorice-flavored pod. Use the entire spice.

Tamarind (imli): The dried black pods of the tamarind plant are sour in taste. Tamarind adds a delicious tang to many dishes. Tamarind pulp has a very long shelf life.

Toor dal: This shiny split lentil is a staple of South India. It is sold as oily and dry. The recipes in this book use dry dal.

Turmeric (haldi): This bright yellow, bitter-tasting spice is sold ground. It is made from a ginger-like rhizome. It provides the characteristic yellow color to Indian curries.

Urad dal: Also known as black gram, this lentil is similar in size to moong dal and is available either with the blackish hull retained or removed. The lentil is creamy white inside. It takes a long time to cook and has a slightly drier texture than moong dal.

Vermicelli: These hair-like noodle strands are made from wheat and are used in savory and sweet dishes.

THE TWO MOST IMPORTANT PARTS TO INDIAN COOKING are the spices and the way those spices are cooked. I am listing here only the techniques that are used in this book. Of course there are many others, such as steaming meat using charcoal, that are not discussed here.

Here is an important tip: remember *mise en place*, or everything in its place. Since many Indian recipes call for multiple ingredients to be added one after another, have all the ingredients ready to go before you start to cook. You will not have time to measure and chop once you have begun to cook.

dry roasting spices

This is an excellent way of extracting the flavors from a spice. The difference in flavor in a spice that has been dry roasted and one that has not is nothing short of dramatic.

Heat a skillet over medium heat. Add the spices whole. Dry roast in the pan for a few minutes until the spices are fragrant, stirring constantly with a wooden spoon to prevent burning. Grind the spices using a mortar and pestle or a coffee/spice mill.

(If you use a coffee grinder, make sure that it is properly cleaned to ensure that none of the spices remain inside. You can clean it by grinding a few tablespoons of rice. I actually have a small grinder reserved just for spices.)

tempering (tadka or baghar)

Many Indian spices are very aromatic and lend their aroma and flavors well to heated oil. Hot oil in turn has the ability to retain and distribute these flavors.

This technique involves heating oil until it is almost smoking, reducing the heat to medium, and then adding the whole spices. Once the spices change color and give off their distinct aromas, remove from the heat and add to the dish. Tadka is added at the beginning or at the end of a dish, depending on the recipe. If the seeds splatter during cooking, never add water.

Common ingredients used in tadka are mustard seeds, cumin seeds, whole red chiles, curry leaves, asafetida, cinnamon sticks, and garlic.

sautéing (bhunao)

Bhunao is actually a combination of sautéing and stir-frying, generally over medium to high heat.

In this technique, used frequently in this book, small amounts of water are added while sautéing to keep the ingredients from sticking or burning. You also need to constantly stir the mixture. Cook and stir until the spice mixture, or masala as it is called, has cooked through and the fat or oil separates out at the sides of the spice mixture. Once this happens, the main ingredients are added to the pan.

roasting (tandoori or bhunna)

In Indian cooking, roasting is usually done in a tandoor oven fired by charcoal. The tandoor imparts a unique smoked flavor to meats, vegetables, and breads. Most Indians do not own tandoors and so most of my recipes have been adapted to the conventional oven or the grill.

INDIAN INGREDIENTS such as ginger garlic paste, garam masala, and paneer are available in most Indian supermarkets. But I have included some recipes here for folks who want to make them themselves. These recipes make small batches.

. . . .

basic recipes

This Indian cottage cheese is very versatile, showing up in snacks, curries, and even desserts. I owe this recipe to a friend in Cleveland.

paneer

. . . .

16 cups / 4 L 1% milk   Juice of 1 lemon
1 cup / 250 mL skim milk powder

IN a large pot, combine the milk and milk powder. Bring to a boil. Stir in the lemon juice. The mixture will start to curdle as it returns to a boil. Remove from the heat. Line a colander with several layers of cheesecloth and place it over a large bowl. Strain the milk, allowing all the whey to drain out. Pull up the corners of the cheesecloth and squeeze the paneer to force out any remaining whey. ✳ Fold up the corners of the cheesecloth to wrap the paneer and place a heavy weight (like a deep pan filled with water) over the paneer to push out any excess moisture and give it some shape. Leave for 2 to 3 hours. ✳ Remove the cloth. Wrap the paneer in plastic wrap. ✳ Paneer keeps for about a week uncooked; if cooked, it keeps for 8 to 10 days. ✳ Many recipes require that you deep-fry the paneer. I recommend that you bake it for 6 to 8 minutes in a 400°F / 200°C oven instead, then use in the recipe. ✳ MAKES: About 12 ounces / 375 g (or 1 generous cup / 300 mL cubes)

This spice blend is a staple in many Indian recipes. Literally translated, it means hot spice mix. You can buy it, but I prefer to make my own, since it really does taste different. Experiment with the quantity of the ingredients to find what works best for you.

garam masala

. . . .

3 black cardamom pods   8 whole cloves
3 green cardamom pods   4 teaspoons / 20 mL cumin seeds
1 (3-inch / 8-cm) cinnamon stick

DRY roast the spices in a skillet over medium heat, stirring constantly, until fragrant. Let cool. Grind in a coffee/spice mill. Store in an airtight jar. ✳ MAKES: About 2 tablespoons / 25 mL

chaat masala

. . . .

1 tablespoon / 15 mL cumin seeds
1 tablespoon / 15 mL coriander seeds
2 teaspoons / 10 mL dried mint
Pinch of asafetida

1 teaspoon / 5 mL ground ginger
1 teaspoon / 5 mL mango powder
1 teaspoon / 5 mL rock salt

IN a skillet over medium heat, dry roast the cumin seeds, coriander seeds, mint, and asafetida until fragrant. Remove from the heat and stir in the ginger, mango powder, and rock salt. Grind in a coffee/spice mill. Store in an airtight jar. ✳ MAKES: About 3 tablespoons / 45 mL

ginger garlic paste

. . . .

Equal amounts of ginger and garlic
   (peeled)

Few green chiles (optional)

IN a blender, grind together the ginger, garlic, and green chiles to form a smooth paste. Store in an airtight jar in the fridge for up to 2 months (or freeze).

besan bundi

. . . .

½ cup / 125 mL chickpea flour
Salt to taste

Water
Oil for frying

In a bowl mix the chickpea flour with salt and enough water to make a thick batter. ✳ Heat the oil in a large saucepan over medium heat. When it is hot but not smoking (test by adding 1 or 2 drops of the flour mixture; if it immediately floats to the surface, the oil is ready), press the batter through a colander or slotted spoon with large holes (about ¼ inch / 5 mm in diameter) into the oil. Fry until the balls are crisp and deep yellow, about 2 or 3 minutes. Drain the balls on paper towels and let cool. Store in an airtight container for up to 1 month.

Commercially available chaat masala is quite delicious and will save you time as well. However, if you want to make it yourself, here is a simple recipe.

I often make enough of this useful paste to last me a few weeks. It keeps well in the fridge. You can also buy it at your local Indian grocery store.

These pearl-shaped, savory fun little snacks are often added to whipped yogurt as a quick side dish.

Yogurt is a great way to get your calcium. This method removes the liquid from yogurt, giving it a rich creamy consistency.

hung yogurt

. . . .

1 ¼ cups / 300 mL fat-free plain yogurt

LINE a sieve with several layers of cheesecloth or a paper coffee filter. Place the yogurt in the sieve. If using cheesecloth, tie the ends of the cheesecloth to form a pouch. Place a weight on the yogurt. Let drain for about 1 hour. If using a coffee filter, simply let the liquid drain out. ✳ MAKES: About 1 cup / 250 mL

IN INDIA, SEAFOOD IS THE JEWEL OF GOA, a state on the shores of western India, a place with beautiful palm trees, picture-perfect sun-drenched beaches, and sunsets to die for. Goan cuisine is influenced by the Portuguese settlers of the 1500s. The dishes are aromatic with strong flavors that delight the palate. Goan food is often referred to as the ambrosial fare of India. ❊ The following menu highlights some of my Goan favorites. I have made a few changes to the traditional recipes to make them healthier. Substitute your own favorite fish. Goan leftovers are wonderful, dare I say sometimes tasting better than the original dish! ❊ If you're serving the baked fish by itself, serve some warm store-brought pitas with it, lightly brushed with your favorite herb or spice butter.

Serves 4
—❊—

bottoms up

getting started

where's the real food?

on the side

live a little

heavenly leftovers

◈ = EXPRESS MENU

seafood sunday

Panna gets its name from the Hindi word for emerald, as the color of this drink is a dusky green. This emerald green juice is really refreshing on hot summer days. It will keep in the refrigerator for about a week.

Tips: This drink tastes better if you let it sit overnight.

raw mango juice (panna)

Prep Time: 5 minutes
Cooking Time: 30 minutes

1 unripe mango
2½ cups / 625 mL water
2 tablespoons / 25 mL sugar

¼ teaspoon / 1 mL grated fresh ginger
Pinch of salt

PEEL the mango and cut the pulp into small pieces. In a deep saucepan, boil the mango with 1 cup / 250 mL of the water and the sugar until the mango pieces are soft, about 15 minutes. Let cool. ❋ In a blender, purée the pulp with the remaining 1½ cups / 375 mL of water, the ginger and salt. Serve chilled with a slice of lime. ❋ VARIATIONS: Add 1 teaspoon / 5 mL lemon juice. Or add fresh mint leaves or a pinch of nutmeg. ❋ A friend tried this recipe using kiwi. His advice is to roast the kiwi (3 per mango) in a 120°F / 50°C oven for about 10 minutes, until the skin is soft. In addition to the ginger, he adds ¼ cup / 60 mL finely chopped mint leaves, 2 tablespoons / 25 mL lemon juice and a pinch of rock salt. Everything goes in the blender along with 2 cups / 500 mL ice water.
EACH SERVING PROVIDES: CALORIES: 41; PROTEIN: TRACE; CARBOHYDRATES: 10 G; FAT: TRACE

Mussels are not commonly eaten in India. I learnt how to make these when I was growing up in Bahrain, an island in the Arabian Gulf. You can create a spectacular presentation by arranging these on a pretty serving platter surrounded by beautiful vegetable garnishes.

Tips: If pastry shells are not available, serve on warm toasted French bread.

mussels in a hat

Prep Time: 15 minutes
Cooking Time: 10 minutes

2 tablespoons / 25 mL vegetable oil
1 small onion, finely chopped
1 small vine-ripened tomato, finely chopped
2 or 3 green chiles, finely chopped
1 pound / 500 g mussels, steamed and finely chopped (see below)

2 teaspoons / 10 mL vinegar
Salt and pepper to taste
For Hat: 8 frozen mini (1-inch / 2.5-cm) phyllo pastry shells
Garnish: Finely chopped fresh coriander

HEAT the oil in a large saucepan over high heat. Sauté the onions until golden brown (2 to 3 minutes). Add the tomato and the chiles; sauté for 2 to 3 minutes. Add the mussels, vinegar, salt and pepper; sauté for 2 to 3 minutes. ❋ To serve: Cook the pastry shells according to the instructions on the box. Add a teaspoon of the mussel mixture to each pastry shell. Garnish with finely chopped coriander. ❋ VARIATIONS: You can use shrimp instead of mussels. ❋ STEAMING MUSSELS: Scrub the mussels clean and pull off the "beard." Discard any mussels that do not close when you handle them and any with broken shells. Fill a large pot with mussels. Do not add water, as the mussels themselves produce all the water needed for steaming. Cook over medium-high heat until all or most of the mussels open (about 3 to 4 minutes). Do not overcook. Discard any that do not open.
EACH SERVING PROVIDES: CALORIES: 120; PROTEIN: 12 G; CARBOHYDRATES: 3 G; FAT: 6 G

roasted lentil wafers (papads)*

Prep Time: None
Cooking Time: 8 minutes

. . . .

8 papads or Indian lentil wafers

THERE are two ways to cook papads. To microwave them, place 1 wafer in the microwave. Cook on high for 1 minute. It is done when little bubbles appear on the surface and the color changes from pale yellow to dark yellow. (You may need to vary the timing a little depending on the strength of your microwave.) ✳ Or you can grill papads. Using tongs, roast each papad lightly on each side. It is done when little bubbles appear on the surface and the color changes from pale yellow to dark yellow. ✳ VARIATIONS: Serve with your choice of chutney as a dipping sauce. There are innovative ways to serve papads given throughout this book!

EACH SERVING PROVIDES (2 PAPADS PER SERVING): CALORIES: 43; PROTEIN: 3 G; CARBOHYDRATES: 8 G; FAT: TRACE

WEB BITES | Order papads online from:
http://www.namaste.com

baked fish (dum macchi)*

Prep Time: 15 minutes; 3 hours for marinating
Cooking Time: 20 minutes

. . . .

2 teaspoons / 10 mL finely chopped
  fresh ginger
2 to 4 cloves garlic, peeled
1 green chile
¼ cup / 60 mL fat-free plain yogurt,
  whipped
¼ cup / 60 mL lemon juice
1 ½ tablespoons / 20 mL vegetable oil

1 tablespoon / 15 mL garam masala
1 teaspoon / 5 mL cumin seeds
½ teaspoon / 2 mL turmeric
½ teaspoon / 2 mL red chile powder
Salt to taste
4 fillets catfish (or any whitefish of your
  choice), about 1 pound / 500 g total
Garnish: Finely chopped fresh coriander

IN a blender, grind the ginger, garlic, and green chile to a smooth paste. In a shallow dish large enough to hold the fish, blend the ginger paste with the yogurt, lemon juice, oil, garam masala, cumin, turmeric, chile powder, and salt. ✳ Cut shallow slits in the fillet to let the marinade sink in. Add the fish to the marinade, turning to coat. Cover and refrigerate for 3 hours. ✳ Preheat the oven to 350°F / 180°C. Place the fish fillets and marinade on a piece of foil on a baking sheet. Fold the foil over the fish and seal the edges (like you were wrapping a present). Bake for 8 to 10 minutes or until the fish is flaky. ✳ Garnish with coriander before serving.

EACH SERVING PROVIDES: CALORIES: 175; PROTEIN: 27 G; CARBOHYDRATES: 3 G; FAT: 6 G

To make these fat-free snacks from scratch you would need a lifetime of practice! Fortunately, excellent papads are readily available at any Indian grocery store or mail-order shop. Be sure to buy the lentil wafers if you want to cook them in the microwave. There are various other kinds (potato wafers, for example) that taste good only if they are deep-fried.

My father used to make this all the time when we were growing up. Every Friday he went to the fish market in Bahrain to buy the most beautiful hamoor (a local fish) that he could find. The fishmongers were kind enough to clean it for us, removing the bones and the skin.

Tips: If you baste the fish with lemon juice first, you will get rid of any fishy smells.

When I first started making this dish, I used regular coconut milk. It tasted wonderful but was so high in fat that I felt guilty each time we ate it! Quite by chance I discovered light coconut milk. Voila! The results are delicious and the fat is limited.

Tips: Pure coconut milk is extremely high in saturated fat. If you decide to use it, do so sparingly to get the flavor minus the fat.

I first ate this at my aunt Nita's house. It was love at first bite! She graciously agreed to let me use her recipe in this book. Although this is a simple dish, it is quite savory, so give it a try.

shrimp in coconut milk (jhinga curry)*

Prep Time: 15 minutes
Cooking Time: 20 minutes

2 tablespoons / 25 mL vegetable oil
1 teaspoon / 5 mL mustard seeds
Leaves from 3 sprigs of curry
1 large tomato, chopped
1-inch / 2.5-cm piece fresh ginger, grated
6 cloves garlic, mashed
2 to 3 green chiles, chopped

1 pound / 500 g shrimp, peeled and deveined
½ teaspoon / 2 mL red chile powder
½ teaspoon / 2 mL turmeric
Salt to taste
¼ cup / 60 mL light coconut milk
½ cup / 125 mL water
Garnish: Finely chopped fresh coriander

In a large saucepan heat the oil over medium heat. Add the mustard seeds; as soon as they crackle add the curry leaves, tomato, ginger, garlic, and green chiles. Sauté gently for 5 minutes or until the tomatoes are soft. Stir in the shrimp; cook for 5 minutes. Add the chile powder, turmeric, and salt; cook for 1 minute. ❊ Add the coconut milk and water. Let the mixture come to a boil, then lower the heat and simmer, stirring occasionally, until the shrimp are tender. ❊ Garnish with the coriander before serving. ❊ VARIATIONS: If you do not like coconut milk, you can replace it with water.
EACH SERVING PROVIDES: CALORIES: 350; PROTEIN: 57 G; CARBOHYDRATES: 2 G; FAT: 12 G

corn and rice pilaf (pullao)*

Prep Time: 5 minutes
Cooking Time: 20 minutes

1 tablespoon / 15 mL vegetable oil
1 tablespoon / 15 mL cumin seeds
1 cup / 250 mL basmati or any
    long-grain rice, rinsed
1 cup / 250 mL corn kernels

1 teaspoon / 5 mL turmeric
Salt to taste
2 cups / 500 mL water
Garnish: Grated carrot and finely chopped
    fresh coriander

In a large saucepan heat the oil over medium heat. Add the cumin seeds. As soon as they splatter add the rice; sauté for 1 minute. ❊ Add the corn, turmeric, salt, and water. Let the mixture come to a boil, then cover and reduce the heat. Cook, without stirring, for 10 minutes or until the rice is cooked through and the water is all dried up. ❊ Serve garnished with grated carrot and chopped coriander. ❊ VARIATIONS: You can use any vegetable or a combination if you do not wish to use corn.
EACH SERVING PROVIDES: CALORIES: 320; PROTEIN: 7 G; CARBOHYDRATES: 64 G; FAT: 4 G

onion salad (raita)

Prep Time: 5 minutes; 1 hour for chilling
Cooking Time: 5 minutes

1 cup / 250 mL hung fat-free plain
   yogurt (page 20)
Pinch of sugar

Salt to taste
1 onion, grated
Garnish: Chopped fresh coriander

PLACE the yogurt in a medium bowl. Add the sugar and salt; mix well. Stir in the onion. Chill for at least 1 hour. Serve garnished with coriander. ❋ VARIATIONS: This is my father-in-law's recipe. Since I like my food a bit on the spicy side, I like to add 2 chopped small green chiles to the salad.
EACH SERVING PROVIDES: CALORIES: 38; PROTEIN: 3 G; CARBOHYDRATES: 6 G; FAT: TRACE

tapioca clouds
(sabudana bahar)

Prep Time: 10 minutes; 3 hours for chilling
Cooking Time: 15 minutes

¼ cup / 60 mL quick-cooking tapioca
½ cup / 125 mL water
1 cinnamon stick
1 ½ cups / 375 mL 1% milk

1 cup / 250 mL low-fat sweetened
   condensed milk
Cloud-shaped mold (optional)
Garnish: Ground cinnamon

IN a medium saucepan, soak the tapioca in the water for 20 minutes. ❋ Add the cinnamon stick, milk, and condensed milk. Cook on medium heat, stirring occasionally, until the tapioca is thick and cooked (about 10 minutes). Test it by picking up a little with a spoon and dropping it on a plate. If it sticks, it is done. Remove the cinnamon stick. ❋ Wet the mold with water and spoon the tapioca into the mold. Chill, covered, for 3 to 4 hours or until firm. When ready to serve, invert the mold onto a plate and gently tap it to loosen the tapioca. Garnish with cinnamon. ❋ VARIATIONS: Add a few drops of vanilla to the uncooked tapioca mixture and leave out the cinnamon.
EACH SERVING PROVIDES: CALORIES: 100; PROTEIN: 7 G; CARBOHYDRATES: 52 G; FAT: 2 G

Believe it or not, in the late B.C. period, onions were forbidden to Hindus seeking a totally religious life. Onions have always been a favorite of mine; they are a true warrior vegetable. They are known to flush toxins from the liver, aid in lowering high blood pressure, and help the digestive system.

My young son loves this dessert. It is mild tasting yet very satisfying.

Tips: If you do not have a mold, use wine glasses and layer the tapioca with light whipping cream. Top with sliced fresh strawberries.

low-fat grilled fish sandwich

. . . .

IF you have some baked fish left over, make this wonderful and tasty low-fat lunch. Warm up the fish in the oven or the microwave. Cut some pocket pita bread in half and place shredded lettuce, chopped tomato, 1 teaspoon / 5 mL low-fat mayonnaise and pieces of the fish inside the pita pocket.

onion toast

. . . .

IF you have any leftover grated onion salad, try this savory guiltless breakfast treat. Take 2 slices of bread. Liberally spread the onion salad on one slice. Sprinkle with the seasoning of your choice (I recommend black pepper); cover with the other slice. Lightly butter the outer sides of the bread. On a hot griddle lightly toast on both sides. Serve warm.

I AM NOT A TRADITIONALIST AND NEVER HAVE BEEN. So it will be no surprise to those who know me to see this section, which provides some nontraditional Indian recipes. The traditional recipes have stood the test of time, and the new ones have stood the test of my pregnancy (when I was an exceedingly picky eater!). ❋ Don't be afraid of the Lentil Dumplings because they are deep-fried. Make a small batch and serve them as a side dish. The idea here is to eat a little of everything, not deprive yourself. ❋ Pick either the cooler (on a hot day) or the tomato soup (on a cold winter night).

Serves 6
— ❋ —

let's try indian
❋

◈ = EXPRESS MENU

The best jal jeera I have ever had was on the back roads of Old Delhi. The vendor shared his secret with me (for a cost, of course!): a pinch of black salt and a lot of practice, he said, will bring out vibrant flavor. He was 92 and had been selling his drink since he was 8 years old — in the same place for over 80 years.

A pregnant friend was over one evening and wanted something spicy to eat. But with her enhanced sense of smell, the smell of strong spices was driving her nuts. So this was what we came up with. Now her daughter enjoys it with her.

mint and ginger cooler (jal jeera)**

Prep Time: 5 minutes
Cooking Time: 10 minutes

2 tablespoons / 25 mL cumin seeds
1 ½ tablespoons / 20 mL dried mint
2 teaspoons / 10 mL mango powder
1 teaspoon / 5 mL ground ginger
2 whole cloves

3 teaspoons / 15 mL coriander paste (see below)
6 teaspoons / 25 mL mint paste (see below)
1 ½ teaspoons / 7 mL sugar
Black salt to taste
Garnish: Lemon slices and fresh mint leaves

IN a skillet over medium heat, toast the cumin, mint, mango powder, ginger, and cloves, stirring constantly, until they smell fragrant (about 45 seconds). Let cool, then blend to a powder in a coffee/spice mill. Store in an airtight jar. ✳ When ready to serve the drink, pour ice water into small juice glasses. To each glass add 1 teaspoon / 5 mL of the spice powder, ½ teaspoon / 2 mL coriander paste, 1 teaspoon / 5 mL mint paste, ¼ teaspoon / 1 mL sugar, and salt. Stir well. ✳ Garnish with a slice of lemon and fresh mint leaves. ✳ VARIATIONS: You can replace the coriander and mint pastes with ½ teaspoon / 2 mL each of Coriander Chutney (page 75) and Mint Chutney (page 76). Instead of mint leaves as a garnish, use an old Indian favorite, besan bundi. These are small fried drops of gram (chickpea) flour. They look like beautiful little pearls. Use 5 or 6 per glass. These are readily available at most Indian grocery stores. If you would like to try your hand at making them, see the recipe on page 19. ✳ TO MAKE CORIANDER PASTE AND MINT PASTE: Blend about 2 tablespoons / 25 mL of fresh leaves with a few drops of water until smooth, about 1 minute. Add a few drops more water to make blending easier if necessary.
EACH SERVING PROVIDES: CALORIES: 8; PROTEIN: 0 G; CARBOHYDRATES: 1 G; FAT: 0 G

honey-glazed chicken*

Prep Time: 4 hours, including marinating
Cooking Time: 35 minutes

FOR THE RED CHILE SPICE RUB:
1 red chile (or 1 teaspoon / 5 mL red chile powder)

¼ teaspoon / 1 mL ground ginger
¼ teaspoon / 1 mL mango powder

FOR THE MARINADE:
¼ cup / 60 mL lemon juice
¼ cup / 60 mL honey
2 teaspoons / 10 mL ginger garlic paste

6 drumsticks, skinned
1 tablespoon / 15 mL melted butter

½ teaspoon / 2 mL finely chopped green chile
Salt to taste

Garnish: Julienned fresh ginger

To make the red chile spice rub: In a small bowl or using a mortar and pestle, pound the whole chile. Add the ginger and mango powder; mix well. ❋ To make the marinade, in a large bowl, mix together the lemon juice, honey, ginger garlic paste, green chile, and salt. Cut deep incisions in the chicken. Add the chicken to the marinade. Mix well. Cover and refrigerate for at least 4 hours. ❋ Preheat the oven to 350°F / 180°C. ❋ Place the chicken on a baking sheet. Roast, basting occasionally with the melted butter, for 10 to 12 minutes or until the chicken is no longer pink inside. ❋ Serve hot garnished with ginger. ❋ VARIATIONS: My sister uses the marinade for pieces of paneer (Indian cheese) or tofu. The results are delicious, not to mention easy on the tummy!

EACH SERVING PROVIDES: CALORIES: 178; PROTEIN: 13 G; CARBOHYDRATES: 10 G; FAT: 5 G

spicy coconut tomato soup (saar)**

Prep Time: 5 minutes
Cooking Time: 35 minutes

1 red chile
1-inch / 2.5-cm piece peeled fresh ginger
1½ tablespoons / 20 mL unsweetened desiccated coconut
½ teaspoon / 2 mL cumin seeds
3 large tomatoes, peeled

2½ cups / 625 mL water
1 (14-ounce/ 398-mL) can light coconut milk
1 teaspoon / 5 mL brown sugar (optional)
Salt to taste
Garnish: 2 tablespoons / 25 mL light coconut milk

FOR THE TADKA:
1 tablespoon / 15 mL vegetable oil
Leaves from 2 sprigs of curry

1 teaspoon / 5 mL finely chopped garlic
½ teaspoon / 2 mL mustard seeds

In a blender or with a mortar and pestle, grind together the red chile, ginger, coconut, and cumin seeds to form a paste. In a food processor, blend this paste with the tomatoes. ❋ In a large saucepan over medium-low heat, heat the water and puréed tomatoes, stirring occasionally, for about 10 minutes. As the soup begins to boil, lower the heat. Reserve 2 tablespoons / 25 mL of the coconut milk for the garnish. Add the remaining coconut milk, sugar, and salt. Stir well. Simmer for 5 minutes. Remove from the heat. ❋ To make the tadka, heat the oil in a small saucepan over medium heat. Add the curry leaves, garlic, and mustard seeds. Cook, stirring, until the mustard seeds begin to crackle, about 30 seconds. Remove from the heat and add to the tomato soup. Mix well and simmer for 2 to 3 minutes. ❋ Ladle into soup bowls. Garnish each bowl with a teaspoon of the coconut milk. ❋ VARIATIONS: I often add blanched carrots and spinach for a truly satisfying soup. You can also top with a few croutons if you wish.

EACH SERVING PROVIDES: CALORIES: 123; PROTEIN: 2 G; CARBOHYDRATES: 7 G; FAT: 9 G

Tips: Wash and dry the chicken before cooking it. Make sure you wash any knives, cutting boards, or other utensils that come in contact with raw poultry before using them for other foods.

The credit for this recipe goes to my husband's uncle Shree. He is one of the most meticulous cooks I know, and his food is always, in one word, delicious.

Tips: This dish works best with fresh tomatoes. To peel the tomatoes, bring a pot of water to a boil. Drop the tomatoes in for about a minute. Transfer the tomatoes to a bowl of cold water to cool. Peel the skin.

The humble Indian cottage cheese, or paneer, is one of the most versatile foods. You can make your own or buy it in various forms from your local Indian grocery store.

Tips: Using a wet knife to cut tofu will make the job easier.

cottage cheese cubes and peas in tomato sauce (mattar paneer)*

Prep Time: 20 minutes
Cooking Time: 25 minutes

2 onions, quartered

3 small tomatoes, quartered

1-inch / 2.5-cm piece peeled fresh ginger

6 cloves garlic

1 green chile

1½ tablespoons / 20 mL vegetable oil

½ cup / 125 mL fat-free plain yogurt, whipped

1 pound / 500 g frozen peas

1 teaspoon / 5 mL red chile powder

1 teaspoon / 5 mL ground coriander

½ teaspoon / 2 mL turmeric

Salt to taste

1 cup / 250 mL water

1 cup / 250 mL cubed paneer or firm light tofu

Garnish: Finely chopped fresh coriander and 1 teaspoon / 5 mL garam masala

IN a food processor, purée the onion, tomatoes, ginger, garlic, and green chile. Heat the oil in a deep skillet over medium heat. Add the purée; cook, stirring occasionally, until all the liquid dries up and oil bubbles on the sides of the mixture. ❄ Reduce heat to medium-low. Add the yogurt and cook for 1 minute. Add the peas, chile powder, coriander, turmeric, and salt. Stir well. Cook for 1 minute. Add the water. Cover and cook until the peas are done, about 5 minutes. Add the paneer. Reduce heat to low and cook, uncovered, for 3 to 4 minutes or until the paneer is soft. Cover, reduce the heat, and simmer the paneer for 10 minutes. ❄ Serve sprinkled with coriander and garam masala. ❄ VARIATIONS: My mother makes this dish without the onions but adds 2 tablespoons / 25 mL dried fenugreek leaves (methi leaves), a classic variation on a classic. I have on many occasions used firm light tofu, and it tastes marvelous, if a little bland compared to the original. If you don't have paneer or tofu, use boiled diced potatoes. A good friend of mine adds diced mushrooms along with the peas.

EACH SERVING PROVIDES: CALORIES: 220; PROTEIN: 12 G; CARBOHYDRATES: 16 G; FAT: 6 G

I created this recipe when I was pregnant. I had been craving a black pepper taste and chicken but I could not find anything that tasted right. Finally, after many trials, success!

garam masala and sour cream chicken bake**

Prep Time: 20 minutes
Cooking Time: 45 minutes

6 chicken thighs or drumsticks, skinned

2 tablespoons / 25 mL vegetable oil

1 large onion, thinly sliced

¼ cup / 60 mL fat-free sour cream

¼ cup / 60 mL fat-free plain yogurt

¼ cup / 60 mL lemon juice

2½ teaspoons / 10 mL garam masala

½ teaspoon / 2 mL turmeric

Salt to taste

PREHEAT the oven to 350°F / 180°C. Cut shallow incisions in the chicken to help the spices sink in. ❋ In a large skillet over medium heat, heat the oil. Add the onions and sauté until light brown. Add the chicken and sauté, turning once, until the chicken is half cooked, about 8 minutes. ❋ Meanwhile, in a bowl combine the sour cream, yogurt, lemon juice, garam masala, turmeric, and salt. Mix to a smooth paste. Add the chicken, turning to coat. ❋ Transfer coated chicken to a baking dish. Bake for 20 minutes or until cooked through. ❋ VARIATIONS: If you find garam masala too pungent for your taste, you can use ground white pepper.

EACH SERVING PROVIDES: CALORIES: 141; PROTEIN: 15 G; CARBOHYDRATES: 4 G; FAT: 7 G

coriander layered potatoes
(multani aloo)*

Prep Time: 10 minutes
Cooking Time: 25 minutes

6 potatoes, peeled and thinly sliced
Vegetable cooking spray
1 cup / 250 mL finely chopped
   fresh coriander
2 teaspoons / 10 mL ground coriander

2 teaspoons / 10 mL ground cumin
1 teaspoon / 5 mL red chile powder
1 teaspoon / 5 mL turmeric
Salt to taste
Garnish: Thinly sliced peeled fresh ginger

PREHEAT the oven to 350°F / 180°C. Place the potatoes in a single layer in a roasting pan; spray with the vegetable cooking spray. Bake until potatoes are tender (about 10 minutes, depending on thickness). Remove the potatoes from the oven and let cool. ❋ Meanwhile, in a bowl stir together the fresh coriander, ground coriander, cumin, chile powder, turmeric, and salt. Cover the bottom of a large saucepan with a thin layer of overlapping potatoes; do not leave any gaps. Sprinkle with some of the spice mixture. Continue layering until all the potatoes and spices are used. Sprinkle with a few drops of water. Cover and cook over very low heat for about 8 minutes to release and blend the spice flavors. Check frequently to ensure that the potatoes do not burn. ❋ Serve hot garnished with thinly sliced ginger. ❋ VARIATIONS: My grandmother used to make this dish in the days when deep-frying was not considered evil, and she would deep-fry the potatoes instead of baking them. I have to admit, it did taste awesome!

EACH SERVING PROVIDES: CALORIES: 83; PROTEIN: 2 G; CARBOHYDRATES: 18 G; FAT: TRACE

WEB BITES These sites are full of information on selecting and cooking potatoes:
http://www.ams.usda.gov/howtobuy/potato.htm
http://www.geocities.com/NapaValley/4079/potato.htm
http://www.dole5aday.com/encyclopedia/potato/potato_select.html

Tips: This dish does not freeze well because of the yogurt and sour cream. But it will keep in the fridge for a few days and makes delicious leftovers.

This dish gets its name from the "Multani masala" my grandmother would sprinkle on her potatoes along with some of the spices listed on the left. My attempt to capture the taste here comes pretty close. Multan, a city in Pakistan, is where my family originates from.

Multani masala can be found only in the backstreets of Chandi Chowk, a famous shopping area in Delhi. My grandfather had a store in Chandi Chowk, and he would bring us this masala from his friends there.

I know a number of people will shake their heads when they see a deep-fried dish in a healthy cookbook. But a small helping — which is the way Indians eat anyway — is not only delicious, but contains only 220 calories.

Tips: The dumplings can be fried ahead of time, then frozen for up to 3 months. When you are ready to use them, place them in a bowl of very hot water for 2 to 3 minutes to thaw them.

If you prefer a softer dumpling, add about 1 tablespoon / 15 mL of fat-free plain yogurt to the dumpling mixture before frying.

lentil dumplings in yogurt sauce (dahi vada)

Prep Time: 4 hours, including soaking the dal
Cooking Time: 30 minutes

FOR THE DUMPLINGS:
1 cup / 250 mL moong dal, washed
1 green chile
1-inch / 2.5-cm piece peeled fresh ginger

Pinch of asafetida
Salt to taste

Oil for deep-frying
4 cups / 1 L warm water
1 teaspoon / 5 mL cumin seeds
1 teaspoon / 5 mL red chile powder

Garnish: 2 tablespoons / 25 mL tamarind chutney and 2 tablespoons / 25 mL coriander chutney (optional)

FOR THE YOGURT SAUCE:
2 cups / 500 mL fat-free plain yogurt
¼ cup / 60 mL water

¼ teaspoon / 1 mL salt
¼ teaspoon / 1 mL sugar

SOAK the dal in water for about 3 hours. Drain the dal. In a food processor grind together the dal, green chile, ginger, asafetida, and salt. Add a tablespoon of water to make the blending easier, if necessary. Place the mixture in a bowl and whisk it to incorporate air into it. (This will make the dumplings softer and fluffier.) ❋ Heat the oil in a wok over medium heat. Drop a teaspoon of the dal mixture into the oil; if it rises to the top immediately, the oil is ready. Working in batches and not crowding the dumplings, place a tablespoon / 15 mL of the dal mixture in the oil and fry, turning, until golden brown, about 1 minute. Drain the dumplings on paper towels. Repeat until all the dal mixture is used up. ❋ Soak the dumplings in a bowl of hot water for 10 minutes. ❋ Meanwhile, make the yogurt sauce. In a medium bowl whisk together the yogurt, water, salt, and sugar until smooth. ❋ Drain the dumplings. Squeeze each one between the palms of your hands to remove excess water. ❋ In a small skillet over medium heat, toast the cumin seeds, stirring frequently, until fragrant (about a minute). ❋ In a serving dish, arrange the dumplings in rows. Pour the yogurt sauce over the dumplings. Garnish with the cumin seeds, chile powder, and the chutneys, if desired. ❋ VARIATIONS: If you are on a very strict diet that absolutely does not allow for deep-fried foods, use diced boiled potatoes instead of the dumplings. The dumplings in this dish are traditionally made with chickpea flour. To make chickpea flour dumplings, replace the moong dal with 1 cup / 250 mL of chickpea flour; add enough water to make a batter for dropping consistency. Add the remaining ingredients, mix well, and proceed as above.

EACH SERVING PROVIDES: CALORIES: 220; PROTEIN: 14 G; CARBOHYDRATES: 31 G; FAT: 7 G

indian flat bread (tandoori naan)

Prep Time: 3 hours
Cooking Time: 20 minutes

½ cup / 125 mL warm water
½ teaspoon / 2 mL sugar
¼ teaspoon / 1 mL salt
¼ teaspoon / 1 mL yeast
2 cups / 500 mL all-purpose flour
1 teaspoon / 5 mL baking powder

1 teaspoon / 5 mL baking soda
1 egg
¼ cup / 60 mL skim milk
1 teaspoon / 5 mL melted butter
¼ teaspoon / 1 mL onion seeds (optional)

PUT the water in a small bowl. Add the sugar, salt, and yeast. Stir until the sugar is dissolved. Set aside for a few minutes until the yeast begins to foam. ❊ In a mixing bowl, sieve the flour, baking powder, and baking soda. In a small bowl, whisk together the egg and milk. Gradually knead the liquid into the flour. Begin adding the yeast mixture while kneading. Knead until the dough is smooth and does not stick to the bowl (about 5 minutes). Brush the dough lightly with the melted butter. Cover with a moist cloth and leave in a warm place until the dough has doubled (about 2 to 3 hours). ❊ Preheat the oven to 350°F / 180°C. Divide the dough into 8 to 10 balls and place on a lightly floured surface. Flatten each ball with your hand into a 6-inch / 15-cm circle. A true naan looks like a teardrop, so stretch one side to elongate it. ❊ Place on a nonstick baking sheet and sprinkle with the onion seeds, if desired. Bake for 3 to 4 minutes or until small darkish bubbles appear on the surface. ❊ Serve immediately, or wrap in foil and reheat in a 300°F / 150°C oven until warmed through. ❊ VARIATIONS: If the weather is hot, you can omit the yeast and let the dough rise on its own. When you serve the naan, brush it slightly with Indian spice butter for a savory taste. Spice butter is easy to make. Take a stick of butter (½ cup / 125 mL) at room temperature. Add about a teaspoon of your favorite dried ground spice (ground cumin, crushed garlic, etc.). Blend well and chill. You can also brush the naan with a little garlic butter for a tasty snack. ❊ MAKES: 10
EACH SERVING PROVIDES: CALORIES: 191; PROTEIN: 6 G; CARBOHYDRATES: 38 G; FAT: 2 G

A tandoor is an open clay oven whose heat is provided by charcoal. Tandoori cooking hails from northwestern India, where the tandoor is used to grill meats and bake bread. Meats cooked in the tandoor are amazingly succulent.

Tips: Authentic naan has the shape of a teardrop, because of the way the dough droops when it is applied to the wall of a tandoor for baking.

Do not use a rolling pin, which will flatten out the air bubbles in the dough, preventing the naan from rising.

One trick is to sprinkle a few drops of water on the naan before putting it in the oven. When it's cooked, all the places that had water droplets will be black.

Store naan in an airtight container in the refrigerator for about a week.

How do you know whether your rice has been cooked to perfection? As my mother would say, each grain should lie separately. This is one traditional recipe that has weathered the changing tastes of our family.

Tips: A few drops of lemon juice added when the water begins to boil will make the rice fluffier and whiter.

This recipe was an open secret among our friends in Bahrain. I heard an advertisement on TV the other night that described this dish perfectly: "Sunday taste, Tuesday effort"!

Tips: Before serving, dip the ice-cream mold in warm water to make it easier to remove the ice cream.

white rice inspiration (jeera chawal)

Prep Time: 30 minutes
Cooking Time: 20 minutes

1 ½ cups / 375 mL basmati rice, soaked in water for 30 minutes
1 tablespoon / 15 mL vegetable oil
1 teaspoon / 5 mL cumin seeds
1 small onion, finely chopped
3 whole cloves
3 bay leaves
2 cinnamon sticks
Salt to taste
3 cups / 750 mL water
8 to 10 pearl onions, boiled and peeled

DRAIN the rice. Heat the oil in a large saucepan over medium heat. Add the cumin seeds and onions; sauté for 1 minute. Stir in the cloves, bay leaves, cinnamon, and rice; sauté for another 2 minutes. Add the salt and water. Bring to a boil, reduce the heat, and cook, covered, for 10 minutes. ❉ Place the pearl onions on top of the rice. Cook, covered, for another 5 minutes or until the water dries up. ❉ Remove the bay leaves and cinnamon stick. Serve warm. ❉ VARIATIONS: Replace the chopped onion with your choice of vegetable. For extra flavor, use chicken stock instead of water.

EACH SERVING PROVIDES: CALORIES: 264; PROTEIN: 5 G; CARBOHYDRATES: 52 G; FAT: 4 G

no-cook indian ice cream (kulfi)

Prep Time: 5 minutes
Cooking Time: Need to freeze overnight

1 (14-ounce / 398-mL) can fat-free evaporated milk
1 (14-ounce / 398-mL) can sweetened low-fat condensed milk
1 cup / 250 mL low-fat heavy cream
2 teaspoons / 10 mL ground cardamom (optional)
Garnish: A few drops of rose water

IN a large bowl, stir together well the evaporated milk, condensed milk, cream, and cardamom. Pour into popsicle molds, Indian stainless steel kulfi molds, or even a small bowl. Freeze overnight. Remove from the molds. Serve sprinkled with rose water. ❉ VARIATIONS: The possibilities are endless. Instead of the cardamom, you can add your own favorite flavoring. I love crushed unsalted pistachios. Another favorite is ¼ cup / 60 mL of mango pulp. My sister loves hers plain topped with crushed almonds. In most Indian grocery stores you will find a delicious rose syrup called Rooh Afsa; top each serving with a teaspoonful. ❉ MAKES: 12 pieces

EACH SERVING PROVIDES: CALORIES: 180; PROTEIN: 5 G; CARBOHYDRATES: 30 G; FAT: 4 G

potato sandwiches

· ·

IF you have any potatoes left over, toast some bread (or leftover naan), place some of the warmed potatoes on the bread, and top with a teaspoon of finely chopped onion.

boiled egg treats

· ·

THIS is a really nifty use for any leftover curries. If you have any curry left over from the Cottage Cheese and Peas, warm it slightly. Boil 2 eggs. Halve the eggs. Place them on a plate and pour the curry on the eggs. Serve with leftover naan or toasted bread.

IN INDIA WE WATCH CRICKET. I once told an American friend that cricket was the right way to play baseball. I have not seen him since! ❋ A dear friend in Cleveland always hosted Super Bowl parties. Not being a big pizza fan, I would always bring Wheels of Fortune (pancakes with chutney). It took a while for me to get the guys to try something different. The biggest challenge was the Mixed Nut Cooler versus beer. No prize for guessing who won there. ❋ This menu was a true test of East meets West. I have served the Shrimp Sachets side by side with Buffalo wings, and the Mango and Cucumber Salad with corn chips.

Serves 6

an indian super bowl party

◈ = EXPRESS MENU

The Moguls brought almonds to Indian cooking. Almonds give any dish a sense of luxury. If you ever visit Delhi, try the thandai at Haldirams, one of the city's most famous eating joints. It is simply awesome.

Rose essence is sold at Indian grocery stores. If you can't find it, use 1 table-spoon / 15 mL rose water, available at many supermarkets.

Tips: To blanch almonds: Place the shelled almonds in a pot of water and bring to a boil. Turn off the heat and let stand for 20 minutes. Drain nuts and spread out on a towel to dry. The skins will slip off easily.

mixed nut cooler (thandai)

Prep: 10 minutes, not including chilling
Cooking Time: None

2 cups / 500 mL skim milk
1 (14-ounce / 398-mL) can fat-free evaporated milk
10 blanched almonds
3 cardamom pods, bruised
2 tablespoons / 25 mL sugar
2 teaspoons / 10 mL fennel seeds

1 teaspoon / 5 mL poppy seeds, soaked in warm water for 5 minutes
1 teaspoon / 5 mL peppercorns
A few threads of saffron
A few drops of rose essence (optional)
Garnish: Crushed ice and red rose petals

PUT 1 cup / 250 mL of the skim milk in a blender. Add the evaporated milk, almonds, cardamom pods, sugar, fennel, poppy seeds, peppercorns, saffron, and rose essence. Blend until smooth. Pass the mix through a sieve lined with cheesecloth. Stir in the rest of the skim milk and mix well. Refrigerate for a few hours. ❄ Serve in tall chilled wine glasses over crushed ice. Drop a few red rose petals in the glass. ❄ VARIATIONS: Many relatives of mine add cashew nuts to this drink. One friend has added a shot of Bailey's and claims that it tastes out of this world. I will leave that up to you!
EACH SERVING PROVIDES: CALORIES: 100; PROTEIN: 6 G; CARBOHYDRATES: 16 G; FAT: 2 G

WEB BITES | This site has some good information on blanching nuts:
http://www.msue.msu.edu/imp/mod01/01600659.html

savory indian wafers with potatoes and onions (stuffed papad)*

Prep Time: 20 minutes
Cooking Time: 8 minutes

. . . .

4 small potatoes, boiled
1 tablespoon / 15 mL vegetable oil
1 teaspoon / 5 mL mustard seeds
1 teaspoon / 5 mL cumin seeds
1 whole red chile, crushed
Leaves from 2 sprigs of curry
1 small onion, finely chopped

2 green chiles, finely chopped
1-inch / 2.5-cm piece ginger, peeled
    and grated
½ teaspoon / 2 mL turmeric
Salt to taste
6 lentil papads

PEEL the potatoes and cut them into very small cubes. ❋ In a large saucepan over medium heat, heat the oil. Add the mustard seeds, cumin seeds, red chile, and curry leaves. As soon as the mustard seeds splatter, add the onions, green chiles, and ginger. Sauté for a few minutes, until the onions are soft. Stir in the turmeric and salt. Cook for another minute. Add the potatoes. Cook, stirring occasionally, for 5 minutes or until the onions are cooked through. Let cool. ❋ Lightly wet a papad with water. Place one-sixth (1 generous table-spoon / 20 mL) of the onion mixture on the left side of the papad. Fold the papad into a semi-circle and seal the edge with a toothpick. Continue with remaining papads and filling. ❋ When you are ready to serve, heat each papad in the microwave for 1 minute or until the filling is hot and the papad is dark yellow. ❋ VARIATIONS: You can stuff the papads with any leftover vegetables (the key is that the filling should be dry). If you are not worried about caloric intake, you can even deep-fry the filled papads.

EACH SERVING PROVIDES: CALORIES: 103; PROTEIN: 4 G; CARBOHYDRATES: 16 G; FAT: 3 G

It may take some practice to ensure that the papads do not break when you stuff them. It really is worth the effort, though — they're delectable.

Tips: Make sure you buy papads that can be roasted or microwaved. There are a few varieties that can only be deep-fried.

I used to make these all the time with paneer. One afternoon I was cooking lunch, made the marinade, and then realized I was out of paneer. Sheer laziness prompted me to try shrimp. I have to say, sometimes even laziness is a good thing.

Tips: You can make the sachets a few hours ahead and keep them in the refrigerator. Heat in the oven just before serving.

When I was in college in Bangalore, a lovely city in southern India, our college canteen (or cafeteria) would serve these. Each time I make these, they bring back memories of a fun and carefree time in my life.

shrimp sachets**

Prep Time: 10 minutes
Cooking Time: 10 minutes

1 pound / 500 g cooked medium shrimp
¼ cup / 60 mL coriander leaves, finely chopped
2 tablespoons / 25 mL ginger garlic paste
2 tablespoons / 25 mL tomato purée
2 tablespoons / 25 mL lemon juice

1 tablespoon / 15 mL vegetable oil
2 teaspoons / 10 mL mango powder
2 teaspoons / 10 mL pomegranate powder
1 ½ teaspoons / 7 mL black salt
1 green chile, finely chopped

PREHEAT the oven to 300°F / 150°C. In a bowl combine the shrimp, coriander, ginger garlic paste, tomato purée, lemon juice, oil, mango powder, pomegranate powder, salt, and green chile. ❊ Cut out 6 circles of aluminum foil each 4 inches / 10 cm in diameter. Place one-sixth of the shrimp in the center of each circle. Pull together the outside of the circle as if you were closing a sachet. Place on a baking sheet. Bake for 8 minutes to allow the flavors to meld. Serve at once. ❊ VARIATIONS: To make Paneer Sachets, replace the shrimp with ¼ cup / 60 mL of paneer or extra-firm tofu cut into small cubes.
EACH SERVING PROVIDES: CALORIES: 133; PROTEIN: 20 G; CARBOHYDRATES: 2 G; FAT: 4 G

wheels of fortune: spicy indian pancakes with coriander chutney (uttapams)**

Prep Time: 45 minutes, including standing time
Cooking Time: 20 minutes

FOR THE TOPPING:
1 small onion, finely chopped
1 tomato, finely chopped
1 green chile, chopped

Handful of coriander leaves, finely chopped
1 teaspoon / 5 mL finely grated ginger

FOR THE BATTER:
¾ cup / 175 mL rice flour
¾ cup / 175 mL semolina (sooji)
½ cup / 125 mL fat-free plain yogurt, whipped

¼ cup / 60 mL (approx.) vegetable oil

1 teaspoon / 5 mL ENO Fruit Salt or baking powder
Salt to taste

Coriander Chutney (page 75)

To make the topping: In a bowl, mix together the onion, tomato, chile, coriander, and ginger; set aside. ❈ To make the batter: In another bowl, stir together the rice flour, semolina, yogurt, ENO Fruit Salt, and salt. Add enough water to make a smooth, pourable batter, similar to pancake batter. Set aside for 30 minutes. ❈ Heat a small nonstick skillet over medium-high heat. Sprinkle on a few drops of water; if they sizzle, the pan is ready. Add a teaspoon of oil and smear the skillet (use very little oil or the batter will stick). Lower the heat to medium-low. ❈ Pour about 3 tablespoons / 45 mL of batter into the skillet. The pancake should be about ¼ inch / 5 mm thick. ❈ When bubbles appear on the surface, spread a tablespoonful of the vegetable mixture evenly over the pancake. Pour a teaspoon / 5 mL of oil along the sides as well. When the underside is golden, carefully turn the pancake over and cook the other side until done (about a minute). Transfer to a serving platter and cook the remaining five uttapams. ❈ Serve hot with Coriander Chutney. ❈ VARIATIONS: I like to add grated paneer and thinly sliced bell peppers to the topping. Also, I have often created Indian pizzas with this pancake as a base. If you do not have semolina, try cream of wheat as a substitute.

EACH SERVING PROVIDES: CALORIES: 217; PROTEIN: 6 G; CARBOHYDRATES: 49 G; FAT: TRACE

chicken rollups*

Prep Time: 25 minutes
Cooking Time: 20 minutes

1 pound / 500 g skinless, boneless chicken breasts, cut into thin strips
½ teaspoon / 2 mL cumin seeds
¼ teaspoon / 1 mL ground cloves
1½ tablespoons / 20 mL vegetable oil
1 onion, thinly sliced
1 tomato, finely chopped
2 teaspoons / 10 mL julienned peeled ginger

4 cloves garlic, crushed
1 green chile, finely chopped
1 teaspoon / 5 mL red chile powder
1 teaspoon / 5 mL turmeric
Salt to taste
6 soft fat-free tortillas
1 egg, beaten

IN a large saucepan of water, bring the chicken, cumin seeds, and cloves to a boil. Boil until the chicken is tender (about 10 minutes or less). Drain the chicken and set aside. ❈ In a nonstick pan, heat the oil over medium heat. Add the onion and sauté until golden. Add the tomato, ginger, garlic, and green chile. Sauté for 3 to 4 minutes or until the tomatoes are soft. Add 2 tablespoons / 25 mL water to keep the mixture from sticking to the pan. Cook until all the liquid dries up. ❈ The masala (as this mixture is called) is done when the

Tips: ENO Fruit Salt is actually an antacid used in India, but many cooks use it as a baking agent. You will find it in most Indian grocery stores. Or you can substitute baking powder.

This batter will keep in the fridge for about a week. It does not freeze well.

I learnt to make this recipe from my cousin Alpana. One taste and I was hooked. One time for a college fundraiser in Lynchburg, Virginia, two of my Japanese friends helped me make 300 rollups. They were gone in less than 30 minutes!

Tips: Take care not to overcook the chicken when boiling it, or it will be rubbery.

CONTINUED . . .

oil bubbles on the sides of the mixture. Turn the heat down to medium-low. Add the chile powder, turmeric, salt, and chicken; mix well. Remove from the heat and let cool to room temperature. ✳ When ready to serve, in a nonstick pan over medium heat, heat a tortilla. Smear a small spoonful of the beaten egg on the tortilla. Flip the tortilla over to cook the egg. Transfer the tortilla to a serving plate, egg side up. Place one-sixth of the chicken mixture in the center of the tortilla. Roll the tortilla to close it and secure the ends with a toothpick. Repeat with remaining tortillas and filling. ✳ Serve with tomato ketchup. ✳ VARIATIONS: Indian grocery stores sell the traditional staple chappati, an Indian flatbread. You can use these instead of tortillas. If you are watching your cholesterol, replace the whole egg with two egg whites. If you cannot find fat-free tortillas, try whole wheat ones instead.

EACH SERVING PROVIDES: CALORIES: 214; PROTEIN: 21 G; CARBOHYDRATES: 14 G; FAT: 5 G

WEB BITES | One of my favorite on-line stores for Indian spices and groceries is: http://www.namaste.com

steamed semolina savory cakes (idlies)*

Prep Time: 25 minutes
Cooking Time: 20 minutes

1 cup / 250 mL semolina (sooji)
¾ cup / 175 mL fat-free plain yogurt, whipped
½ cup / 125 mL water
1 teaspoon / 5 mL salt
1 teaspoon / 5 mL ENO Fruit Salt or baking powder

THERE are two ways to make these cakes: steaming or microwaving. ✳ Steaming: In a bowl stir together the semolina, yogurt, water, and salt. The batter should be of pouring consistency. Cover with a wet cloth and set aside for 20 minutes. ✳ Boil water in a steamer large enough to hold 4 (½-cup / 125-mL) bowls. ✳ Stir the ENO into the batter. Pour about 3 tablespoons / 45 mL into each bowl. Steam for 8 to 10 minutes or until a toothpick comes out clean. ✳ Remove the cups from the steamer. Gently loosen the edges with a knife, turn the cakes out, and arrange upright on a serving platter. Repeat with the remaining batter. ✳ Microwaving: On a large plate microwave the semolina on high for 1½ minutes; do not stir. Let cool. In a bowl, stir together the semolina, yogurt, water, and salt. The batter should be of pouring consistency. Cover with a wet cloth and set aside for 20 minutes. ✳ Meanwhile, grease 4 (½-cup / 125-mL) microwave-safe bowls. ✳ Stir the ENO into the batter. Pour 3 tablespoons / 45 mL into each bowl.

This is a Monday-night dish! It does not require a lot of effort, tastes wonderful, and is good for you. It's a wonderful life.

Tips: Always add ENO just before you cook the cakes.

These savory cakes freeze well. Let them thaw, then heat them in the microwave, uncovered, for about a minute. Serve hot.

Microwave, uncovered, on high for 4 minutes or until a toothpick comes out clean. (If you want to place more than 4 bowls in the microwave, for each additional bowl add 1 minute to the cooking time.) ✳ Gently loosen the edges with a knife, turn the cakes out, and arrange upright on a serving platter. Repeat with the remaining batter. ✳ Serve with a chutney of your choice. I recommend the coriander or coconut chutneys on pages 75 and 96. ✳ VARIATIONS: Just before cooking, add a teaspoon / 5 mL of cooked grated carrot or cooked chopped spinach to the spice cakes.

EACH SERVING PROVIDES (3 IDLIES PER SERVING): CALORIES: 146; PROTEIN: 6 G; CARBOHYDRATES: 33 G; FAT: TRACE

WEB BITES | If you cannot find ENO at your local Indian grocer, visit: www.namaste.com

mango and cucumber salad

Prep Time: 10 minutes
Cooking Time: None

4 large jalapeño peppers, seeded
   and minced
2 ripe mangoes, peeled and cubed
2 small cucumbers, diced
1 small onion, diced

2 cloves garlic, minced
2 tablespoons / 25 mL finely chopped
   coriander leaves
Juice of 1 lemon
Salt and pepper to taste

IN a bowl, combine the jalapeño peppers, mango, cucumber, onion, garlic, coriander, lemon juice, and salt and pepper. Chill and serve. ✳ VARIATIONS: You can replace mango with pineapple or kiwi.

EACH SERVING PROVIDES: CALORIES: 50; PROTEIN: TRACE; CARBOHYDRATES: 11 G; FAT: TRACE

Use any leftover salad as salsa with your favorite chips.

Tips: Wear rubber gloves when seeding and chopping fresh chile peppers, because the oils in the pepper can irritate your skin. Avoid contact with your eyes after touching chiles.

My husband prefers the pineapple ginger sauce to the mango ginger sauce. Try both; the contrasting flavors of mango or pineapple and ginger give the sauce a very exotic taste.

Tips: Use a melon baller to create the balls.

fresh fruit in mango ginger sauce

Prep Time: 20 minutes
Cooking Time: 5 minutes

1 cup / 250 mL fresh fruit of your choice	2 overripe mangoes, peeled, cubed,
1 cup / 250 mL honeydew melon balls	and puréed
1 cup / 250 mL watermelon balls	2 teaspoons / 10 mL grated ginger
¼ cup / 60 mL water	2 teaspoons / 10 mL honey

MIX all the fruits in a bowl; set aside. ❊ In a small saucepan, warm the water. Remove from the heat and add the mango purée, ginger, and honey. Mix well. ❊ Serve the fruit with the mango ginger sauce on the side. ❊ VARIATIONS: Instead of the mango ginger sauce, try a pineapple ginger sauce. Use 2 cups / 500 mL of crushed pineapple.
EACH SERVING PROVIDES: CALORIES: 56; PROTEIN: TRACE; CARBOHYDRATES: 12 G; FAT: TRACE

WEB BITES | This site has some good information on cooking with honey:
http://members.aol.com/sweetnessl/usehoney.htm

shrimp rice pilaf with baby vegetables

IF you have any shrimp left over, try this old-time favorite of mine. Soak 1 cup / 250 mL of basmati rice in water for 30 minutes. Drain the rice. In a microwave-safe bowl, cook about ½ cup / 125 mL of frozen baby vegetables according to directions on the packet. Drain the vegetables. ❊ In a large saucepan over medium heat, heat 1 tablespoon / 15 mL of vegetable oil. When the oil is hot, add ½ teaspoon / 2 mL of cumin seeds and the baby vegetables; sauté for 2 minutes. Add the leftover shrimp and sauté for another minute. Add about a teaspoon / 5 mL of salt and the rice. Stir well and sauté for 2 minutes. Add 2 cups / 500 mL of water and bring to a boil. Lower the heat, cover, and cook for 15 minutes or until all the water has dried up and the rice is done. Serve hot.

spicy cakes (dhokla)

THESE are so simple yet so delicious. If you have any leftover semolina savory cakes, place them in a serving dish and microwave on high, uncovered, for about a minute until hot. In a small skillet over medium heat, heat 1 tablespoon / 15 mL of vegetable oil. Add ½ teaspoon / 2 mL mustard seeds, 3 or 4 curry leaves, and 1 crushed red chile. Remove from the heat and pour over the savory cakes. Garnish with chopped coriander leaves and chopped green chiles. Serve immediately.

THIS MENU WAS BORN ON MY SON JAI'S FIRST BIRTHDAY. We had a number of guests from all different ethnic backgrounds, and kids are a hard audience to please. ❊ The food is simple to prepare and easy for children to pick up and eat. If you are preparing these dishes for young children, cut them into small enough sizes. ❊ I usually make the custard with custard powder, and it works well, but you can make it from scratch if you wish. (My son can't tell the difference yet!) ❊ I did not include a fat-free recipe for the cupcakes — why mess with perfection! Jokes aside, if you're watching your fat intake, have just one and share the rest.

. . . .

Serves 6

happy birthday to you

◈ = EXPRESS MENU

You can use canned mango here. Since most canned mango is sweetened, you may not need to add any sugar.

Tips: Lassi has a short shelf life and is best fresh.

This is my mother's all-time favorite drink! Believe it or not, this drink brings back memories of high school exams. Whenever I came home after an exam, my mother would always have one of these ready for me. It was her way of getting me to sit down long enough to tell her how the exam went!

Tips: Use a variety of fun straws in the glasses.

mango magic (lassi)

Prep Time: 5 minutes
Cooking Time: None

1 ½ cups / 375 mL fat-free plain yogurt   1 tablespoon / 15 mL sugar
½ cup / 125 mL mango chunks   5 or 6 ice cubes

PUT the yogurt, mango, sugar, and ice in a blender and blend until smooth. Serve immediately. ❉ VARIATIONS: Try strawberries, raspberries, peaches, or even bananas in place of mango.

EACH SERVING PROVIDES: CALORIES: 234; PROTEIN: 2 G; CARBOHYDRATES: 9 G; FAT: TRACE

midnight beauty

Prep Time: 5 minutes
Cooking Time: None

2 (11-ounce / 355-mL) cans cola   6 scoops low-fat vanilla ice cream
  or your favorite soda

DIVIDE the cola among 6 glasses. Add 1 scoop of ice cream to each glass. Serve immediately. ❉ VARIATIONS: A North American variation on this old Indian favorite is to use root beer instead of cola. ❉ I used Healthy Choice Low-Fat Vanilla Ice Cream for the nutritional analysis.

EACH SERVING PROVIDES: CALORIES: 56; PROTEIN: TRACE; CARBOHYDRATES: 13 G; FAT: TRACE

indian chex mex

Prep Time: 5 minutes
Cooking Time: 5 minutes

FOR THE TADKA:

1 tablespoon / 15 mL vegetable oil	¼ teaspoon / 1 mL mango powder
1 teaspoon / 5 mL ground cumin	¼ teaspoon / 1 mL mustard seeds
1 teaspoon / 5 mL coriander seeds	
2 cups / 500 mL plain cornflakes	Pinch of salt
2 tablespoons / 25 mL peanuts (optional)	Pinch of sugar

TO make the tadka, heat the oil in a large saucepan over medium heat. Stir in the cumin, coriander seeds, mango powder, and mustard seeds. When the mustard seeds start to splatter, remove from the heat. (You can cover with a splatter guard if you wish.) ❊ Add the cornflakes, peanuts, salt, and sugar. Mix well. ❊ VARIATIONS: Add salted pretzels to the mix.

EACH SERVING PROVIDES: CALORIES: 105; PROTEIN: 3 G; CARBOHYDRATES: 10 G; FAT: 6 G

wheels of the bus

Prep Time: 5 minutes
Cooking Time: 5 minutes

1 teaspoon / 5 mL vegetable oil	Salt and pepper to taste
¼ cup / 60 mL grated paneer	A few coriander leaves
1 tomato, sliced	
6 reduced-fat Ritz crackers (or any round crackers of your choice)	

HEAT the oil in a large saucepan over medium-high heat. Sauté the paneer for 2 to 3 minutes. Remove from the heat and let cool. ❊ Place a slice of tomato on each cracker. Top with a teaspoon of paneer. Sprinkle with salt and pepper to taste. Place a single coriander leaf on top and serve. ❊ VARIATIONS: Use your choice of cheese. I have occasionally added a dash of Tabasco when sautéing the paneer.

EACH SERVING PROVIDES: CALORIES: 91; PROTEIN: 5 G; CARBOHYDRATES: 4 G; FAT: 6 G

Each time I make this snack, this picture comes to mind: It is four o'clock on a Sunday afternoon. My father-in-law and mother-in-law are playing cards, sipping their afternoon tea, and enjoying these nibbles.

Tips: This mixture can be stored for about 2 months in an airtight container.

My six-year-old nephew helped me coin the name for these treats.

Tips: You can replace the cracker with the spicy Indian pancakes (uttapams) on page 40. Top with the sliced tomato, uncooked paneer, salt and pepper. Place in a 200°F / 95°C oven for 3 to 4 minutes or until heated through.

Use cookie cutters to cut the bread into different shapes to suit the occasion.

Tips: Kraft fat-free cheese works well in this recipe.

creatures of the sea

Prep Time: 5 minutes
Cooking Time: 5 minutes

6 slices bread, lightly toasted
1 cup / 250 mL baked beans
1 egg, scrambled

¼ cup / 60 mL finely shredded
fat-free cheese
Finely chopped coriander leaves

PREHEAT the oven to 250°F / 120°C. ❋ Use fish-shaped cookie cutters (about 3 or 4 inches / 8 or 10 cm) to cut the bread. In a bowl, combine the beans and the scrambled egg. ❋ Place the bread shapes in an ovenproof dish. Spread about a tablespoon / 15 mL of the bean mixture on the bread. Sprinkle with the cheese. ❋ Bake until the cheese is golden brown (about 5 minutes or less). ❋ Sprinkle with coriander and serve with tomato ketchup. ❋ VARIATIONS: If you have older kids who like a bit of spice, mix about a teaspoon / 5 mL of Tabasco into the beans and serve hot!
EACH SERVING PROVIDES: CALORIES: 107; PROTEIN: 6 G; CARBOHYDRATES: 19 G; FAT: 1 G

WEB BITES

One of the best recipes I know to scramble eggs is on this site: http://www.wholehealthmd.com/refshelf/foods_view/0,1523,98,00.html

I came across this Web site when I was researching eggs; it has some really good egg recipes: http://www.virtualcities.com/ons/0rec/04eggs.htm

This dish is very popular with all my cousins. I often take these to work for a quick and healthy lunch. You can either make your own rotis (page 128) or buy them at an Indian grocery store.

veggie frankies

Prep Time: 20 minutes
Cooking Time: 10 minutes

1 ½ tablespoons / 20 mL vegetable oil
1 small onion, chopped
1 teaspoon / 5 mL cumin seeds
1 teaspoon / 5 mL red chile powder
1 cup / 250 mL shredded cabbage

1 cup / 250 mL finely chopped spinach
½ cup / 125 mL grated carrot
Salt to taste
6 chappatis (rotis)

IN a large nonstick saucepan, heat the oil over medium heat. Add the onion; sauté until golden brown. Stir in the cumin seeds and chile powder. Sauté for about 30 seconds. ❋ Add the cabbage, spinach, and carrot. Cook, covered and stirring occasionally, for 6 minutes or until all the vegetables are tender. If necessary, add a few tablespoons of water to prevent the spices from sticking to the pan. Ensure that all the water dries up. Season with salt. ❋ Warm the chappatis in a dry nonstick skillet over medium heat. ❋ Place one-sixth of the vegetable mixture in the center of each chappati. Roll the chappatis and secure with a toothpick. ✳ Serve warm. ✳ VARIATIONS: You can add mashed potatoes to the filling. A neighbor back in Ohio used to add grated paneer and thinly sliced ginger along with a teaspoon of hot green chile chutney.

EACH SERVING PROVIDES: CALORIES: 130; PROTEIN: 4 G; CARBOHYDRATES: 20 G; FAT: 4 G

WEB BITES | If you don't find flappers at your local grocery store, you can buy them at: http://www.flappers.com

hot dog bowls

Prep Time: 20 minutes
Cooking Time: 10 minutes

1 tablespoon / 15 mL vegetable oil
1 small onion, chopped
¼ cup / 60 mL tomato sauce
1 cup / 250 mL cooked red kidney beans, drained and rinsed if canned

6 small fat-free hot dogs, cooked and sliced
6 small hamburger buns
3 teaspoons / 15 mL butter
Garnish: Grated cheese

IN a medium nonstick saucepan, heat the oil over medium heat. Add the onion; sauté until golden brown. Add the tomato sauce and cook, stirring occasionally, for 2 minutes. Stir in the kidney beans; reduce heat to low and simmer for 4 minutes. Stir in the hot dogs; simmer for another minute. Remove from the heat. ✳ Cut the tops off the buns horizontally. Scoop out the center of the buns, leaving about an inch / 2.5 cm on the sides to form a bread bowl. Lightly butter the insides of each bowl. Place one-sixth of the hot dog mixture inside each bowl. ✳ Serve topped with grated cheese. ✳ VARIATIONS: You can use home-made chili instead of the kidney beans.

EACH SERVING PROVIDES: CALORIES: 201; PROTEIN: 11 G; CARBOHYDRATES: 25 G; FAT: 6 G

Tips: If you don't have chappatis at home, use flappers! Flappers are an old favorite of mine. They are flavored Mexican tortillas.

These are really simple to make and always a hit with kids. There's no Indian element, by the way — I just like them!

Tips: Use canned kidney beans to save cooking time. If you are using dried kidney beans, soak them overnight to reduce the cooking time.

For the hot dogs, try the Oscar Meyer fat-free variety. They are quite delicious even without the fat.

Well, what can I say. I had to include them. They are delicious, a real comfort food.

baby cupcakes

Prep Time: 20 minutes
Cooking Time: 35 minutes

½ cup / 125 mL unsalted butter
½ cup / 125 mL sugar
2 eggs

¾ cup / 175 mL all-purpose flour
1 tablespoon / 15 mL cocoa powder
¼ teaspoon / 1 mL baking powder

PREHEAT the oven to 350°F / 180°C. In a mixing bowl, cream the butter and sugar together until light and fluffy. Add the eggs and continue to beat until well mixed. Sieve the flour, cocoa, and baking powder together. Fold the flour mixture into the batter; mix until smooth. Pour the batter into paper-lined muffin tins, filling halfway. ✳ Bake for 25 minutes or until a toothpick inserted in the center of a cupcake comes out clean. ✳ Remove cupcakes from tin and let cool on a rack. This one does not need frosting! ✳ VARIATIONS: Add a few drops of vanilla to the batter. ✳ MAKES: 12 cupcakes
EACH SERVING PROVIDES: CALORIES: 176; PROTEIN: 3 G; CARBOHYDRATES: 21 G; FAT: 9 G

WEB BITES | Excellent tips on baking with Baking Masters free on-line baking school, with recipes and plenty of baking information:
http://www.bakingmasters.com

One of my personal favorite sites on "Rising to the occasion"!
http://www.inquisitivecook.com

The British introduced custard to Indian cuisine. Serve warm or cold, whichever you prefer.

Tips: To prevent the custard from burning, always cook it on medium heat and stir it constantly.

custard and jelly

Prep Time: 20 minutes, plus 6 hours to chill the jelly
Cooking Time: 35 minutes

1 packet Jell-O, your choice of flavor

FOR THE CUSTARD:
2 tablespoons / 25 mL custard powder
1 tablespoon / 15 mL sugar

2 cups / 500 mL 1% milk

PREPARE the Jell-O according to directions on the packet. Chill it in a shallow baking pan. Once the Jell-O has set, use cookie cutters to cut it into fun shapes. ✳ Meanwhile, make the custard. In a bowl blend the custard powder and sugar. Whisk in 2 tablespoons / 25 mL of the milk to form a smooth paste. ✳ Heat the remaining milk. When the milk is nearly boiling, remove from the heat. Add the custard paste. Stir until the paste is completely dissolved. ✳ Bring the custard to boil over medium-low heat, stirring constantly. Transfer to a bowl and chill for about 4 hours. ✳ To serve, spoon 2 tablespoons / 25 mL of the custard into each of 6 dessert bowls. Top with a few Jell-O shapes. ✳ VARIATIONS: Add chopped fresh fruit or nuts to the custard.

EACH SERVING PROVIDES: CALORIES: 63; PROTEIN: 3 G; CARBOHYDRATES: 12 G; FAT: 1 G

trifle

. . . .

IF you have cupcakes, custard, and jelly left over, try this simple dessert. Layer the bottom of a square dessert dish with crumbled cupcakes. Add a layer of the custard, then a layer of the jelly. Continue to do so until all the leftovers are finished. Top off with a dollop of fat-free whipping cream and a generous helping of fresh fruit.

My husband and I entertain often, and many times the dinners are official. This menu is ideal, since it provides guests with a lot of choice. ❄ As a rule I always ask my guests whether they are allergic to anything or have any dietary restrictions. ❄ I have included some information on Indian spirits. Most well-stocked liquor stores carry Indian beers as well.

. . . .

Serves 6
—❄—

the boss is coming

bottoms up

getting started

where's the real food?

on the side

live a little

heavenly leftovers

◈ = EXPRESS MENU

picy lassi is a great digestive aid and is frequently served with a rich Indian meal. Although you can buy ready-made lassis at Indian grocery stores, this is one recipe I would recommend that you make yourself. The store-bought brands just don't do justice to this wonderful drink.

spicy mint drink (salty lassi)

Prep Time: 5 minutes
Cooking Time: None

1 cup / 250 mL fat-free plain yogurt
1 cup / 250 mL water
1 teaspoon / 5 mL finely chopped mint
    leaves (or ¼ teaspoon / 1 mL dried mint)
Pinch of ground cumin

Pinch of grated ginger
Pinch of salt
Pinch of sugar
5 or 6 ice cubes

PUT the yogurt, water, mint, cumin, ginger, salt, sugar, and ice in a blender. Blend for 30 seconds. Serve immediately. ✳ VARIATIONS: Add some ground black pepper instead of cumin. Garnish with fresh cilantro.
EACH SERVING PROVIDES: CALORIES: 33; PROTEIN: 2 G; CARBOHYDRATES: 2 G; FAT: 0 G

cheers! indian spirits

WINES have been made in India since the time of the Indus civilization, around 2500 B.C. In India, drinking wine was for a long time an elite pastime, reserved only for the high-class snobbish types. Somewhere along the way, Madeira, as the old Indian wine was known, lost its popularity, and Indians became scotch and beer drinkers. It is only recently that wines have come back in a big way to the Indian market. ✳ The Indage Group is bringing back the glorious vineyards of western India and reintroducing the Indian palate to wines made from home-grown grapes. Indian wines today are mostly table wines. Local Indian wines such as the Grover red and white, Chhabri (white wine), and Anarkali (red wine) are all making a comeback. Wines are no longer a luxury afforded only by the rich. ✳ The locals in Goa drink feni, a wine made from cashew nuts. It is strong, but the flavor is awesome. Another local drink is toddy, which is made from palms. Check out http://www.goa-world.net/links/ for more information on feni. ✳ Whisky is the most popular spirit, and many people drink Chivas and Black Label. Indians prefer their scotch on the rocks. ✳ More recently, pubs have sprung up all across the country, and beer is quickly overtaking whisky as the drink of choice. Two brands available in North America are Kingfisher and Taj Mahal. The alcohol content of Indian beer is about 8%.

mushroom caps with spinach filling

Prep Time: 20 minutes
Cooking Time: 35 minutes

. . . .

6 mushrooms
2 tablespoons / 25 mL vegetable oil
1 small onion, chopped

2 green chiles, chopped
1 cup / 250 mL chopped spinach

FOR THE SAUCE:
2 tablespoons / 25 mL butter
2 tablespoons / 25 mL all-purpose flour

1 cup / 250 mL 1% milk
Salt and pepper

Garnish: Shredded mozzarella cheese

CLEAN the mushrooms. Discard the stems. In a nonstick saucepan, heat 1 tablespoon /
15 mL of the oil over medium-high heat. Add the onion; sauté until golden brown. Add the
green chiles; sauté for another minute. Add the spinach; sauté for 2 minutes. Remove from
the heat. ✳ To prepare the sauce: In a nonstick saucepan over low heat, melt the butter.
Add the flour and cook for 2 minutes, stirring constantly. Remove from the heat and slowly
whisk in the milk until well blended. Return to the heat and cook, stirring constantly, for
2 to 3 minutes or until the sauce thickens. Remove from the heat. Add salt and pepper
to taste. Stir in the spinach until well mixed. ✳ Stuff each mushroom cap with a small
spoonful of the spinach mixture. ✳ In a medium skillet over medium heat, heat the remaining 1 tablespoon / 15 mL oil. Sauté the mushrooms for 3 to 4 minutes or until they are
almost cooked. Lower the heat to the lowest setting, cover the pan, and steam the
mushrooms for a few more minutes until they are cooked through. ✳ Top each mushroom
with shredded cheese and serve immediately. ✳ VARIATIONS: For a spicy version of this dish,
omit the white sauce. To the chopped onion, add ¼ teaspoon / 1 mL ground cumin,
¼ teaspoon / 1 mL turmeric, ¼ teaspoon / 1 mL red chile powder, and 2 tablespoons /
25 mL grated paneer. Sauté for 4 minutes.
EACH SERVING PROVIDES: CALORIES: 115; PROTEIN: 3 G; CARBOHYDRATES: 9 G; FAT: 5 G

WEB BITES | Here's a site for those of you who want to become mushroom aficionados:
http://www.gmushrooms.com

Rich in iron, spinach is very popular in Indian cooking. My aunt in Delhi makes this starter all the time. She is always experimenting with the filling, and no two are ever the same.

Tips: Select white mushrooms that are about 1 inch / 2.5 cm in diameter to provide enough space for the filling.

Whenever my husband wanted me to cook this dish, he would say, "Can you make that fish that tastes wonderful with my drink?" You guessed it, he is a whisky drinker, and hence the name Whisky Fish.

Tips: If you are using frozen fish fillets, place the fish in a container, cover with milk, and refrigerate overnight to soak and thaw. Just before starting the recipe, remove the fish from the milk and rinse. This will remove the fishy smell and make the fish taste fresher.

In North India this preparation is called chaat. This dish is quintessentially Indian. Every corner of India has a variation all its own, and each is a winner in its own right.

whisky fish*

Prep Time: 10 minutes, plus 45 minutes standing time
Cooking Time: 10 minutes

3 fillets catfish
1 tablespoon / 15 mL lemon juice
2 green chiles, finely chopped
¼ cup / 60 mL finely chopped fresh coriander
¼ cup / 60 mL fat-free plain yogurt

1 tablespoon / 15 mL ginger garlic paste
2 teaspoons / 10 mL garam masala
1 teaspoon / 5 mL ground cumin
1 teaspoon / 5 mL red chile powder
Salt to taste
Garnish: Chaat masala

WASH and pat dry the fish. Put the fish in a bowl and toss gently with the lemon juice. Set aside for 10 minutes. Cut the fish into 1-inch / 2.5-cm cubes. ※ In a medium bowl, combine the chiles, coriander, yogurt, ginger garlic paste, garam masala, cumin, chile powder, and salt; mix well. Add the fish and turn to coat it well. Marinate, covered and refrigerated, for at least 45 minutes. ※ Meanwhile, preheat the oven to 350°F / 180°C. ※ Place the fish in an ovenproof dish and bake until golden brown (5 to 9 minutes). ※ Serve sprinkled lightly with chaat masala. ※ VARIATIONS: You can also use shrimp, or you can cook a whole fish this way.
EACH SERVING PROVIDES: CALORIES: 75; PROTEIN: 14 G; CARBOHYDRATES: 2 G; FAT: 4 G

WEB BITES | The Catfish Institute has some awesome recipes on cooking — what else — catfish (try their Moroccan recipes): http://www.catfishinstitute.com/index.shtml

pomegranate and spice and everything nice*

Prep Time: 20 minutes
Cooking Time: 5 minutes

3 medium potatoes, boiled, peeled, and diced
2 to 3 green chiles, finely chopped
1 small red onion, chopped
1 cup / 250 mL shelled pomegranate

2 tablespoons / 25 mL lemon juice
1 tablespoon / 15 mL finely chopped fresh coriander
2 teaspoons / 10 mL chaat masala

IN a bowl combine the potatoes, chiles, onion, pomegranate, lemon juice, coriander, and chaat masala. Serve at room temperature. ※ VARIATIONS: You can add chickpeas, kidney beans, or cooked green peas. ※ Panfry the potatoes before adding to the chaat and taste the difference.
EACH SERVING PROVIDES: CALORIES: 80; PROTEIN: 2 G; CARBOHYDRATES: 18 G; FAT: TRACE

herb, rice, and chicken bake (biryani)*

Prep Time: 35 minutes
Cooking Time: 1 hour 15 minutes

. . . .

FOR THE CHICKEN:

1 ½ tablespoons / 20 mL vegetable oil

2 tablespoons / 25 mL whole garam masala

2 tablespoons / 25 mL thinly sliced ginger

1 tablespoon / 15 mL crushed garlic

1 tablespoon / 15 mL poppy seed paste

1 onion, ground to a paste

3 small tomatoes, chopped

2 teaspoons / 10 mL red chile powder

2 teaspoons / 10 mL turmeric

1 cup / 250 mL fat-free plain yogurt

2 pounds / 1 kg chicken pieces

Salt to taste

FOR THE RICE:

2 cups / 500 mL basmati rice, washed, soaked in water for 30 minutes, and drained

5 cups / 1.25 L water

2 cinnamon sticks

6 green cardamom pods, cracked

GARNISHES:

½ teaspoon / 2 mL saffron soaked in ½ cup / 125 mL warm milk

¼ cup / 60 mL fresh coriander leaves, finely chopped

¼ cup / 60 mL fresh mint leaves, finely chopped

¼ cup / 60 mL fried onions

¼ cup / 60 mL raisins

HEAT the oil in a large saucepan over medium-high heat. Add the whole garam masala. When it begins to crackle, add the ginger, garlic, poppy seed paste, and onion paste. Sauté for a few minutes until the onion is golden brown. Stir in the tomatoes. Cook, stirring occasionally, for 5 to 6 minutes or until the tomatoes are soft. ❋ Add the red chile, turmeric, and yogurt; sauté for 1 minute. Add the chicken; cook for 6 minutes. Lower the heat and simmer for 15 minutes or until the chicken is tender and the gravy is very thick. Stir in the salt. Remove from the heat. ❋ In a large saucepan combine the rice, water, cinnamon sticks, and cardamom pods. Bring to a boil, cover, reduce heat to low, and cook until the rice is almost done (about 10 minutes). Drain the rice. ❋ Meanwhile, preheat the oven to 300°F / 150°C. Lightly grease a large casserole dish. ❋ Spread one-third of the rice in the casserole dish. Pour half of the saffron liquid over the rice. Sprinkle with half of the coriander, half of the mint, one-third of the fried onions, and one-third of the raisins. Top with half of the cooked chicken. Repeat the layers a second time, ending with the remaining rice. ❋ Cover the casserole. Bake for 8 to 12 minutes or until any remaining liquid has dried up and the rice is fully cooked. ❋ Garnish with remaining fried onions and raisins and serve immediately. ❋ VARIATIONS: Use pieces of lamb or beef instead of chicken.

CONTINUED . . .

The original Biryani was developed in Hyderabad, a city in South India, by the Nizams, the Mogul rulers of India in the 1500s who were connoisseurs of food, music, and dance. In my opinion, they perfected the art of cooking meat and rice together. This is a humble adaptation of a legendary dish.

Many folks use a variety of vegetables of their choice. I sometimes make this dish with leftover chicken curry. Heat the curry, add desired quantity of uncooked rice, and add about 2 cups / 500 mL water (to ensure that rice has enough liquid to cook). Cover and bake until rice is tender (about 20 minutes).

EACH SERVING PROVIDES: CALORIES: 480; PROTEIN: 50 G; CARBOHYDRATES: 63 G; FAT: 5 G

M asoor dal, the lentils used in this recipe, are red but turn a magnificent golden yellow when cooked.

Tips: Soaking the dal (lentils) in hot water for about an hour before cooking will reduce the cooking time.

Adding turmeric to the dal when it is cooking also shortens the cooking time.

stir-fried dried lentils**

Prep Time: 30 minutes
Cooking Time: 20 minutes

1 tablespoon / 15 mL vegetable oil
¼ teaspoon / 1 mL mustard seeds
1-inch / 2.5-cm piece peeled fresh ginger, thinly sliced
2 green chiles, finely chopped
½ cup / 125 mL thinly sliced onion

¼ cup / 60 mL dried fenugreek leaves, soaked in hot water for 30 minutes and drained
1 teaspoon / 5 mL red chile powder
¼ teaspoon / 1 mL asafetida
¼ teaspoon / 1 mL turmeric
Salt to taste

FOR THE DAL (LENTILS):
½ cup / 125 mL masoor dal (lentils)
2 cups / 500 mL water

¼ teaspoon / 1 mL turmeric
1 tablespoon / 15 mL lemon juice

Garnish: Julienned fresh ginger

HEAT the oil in a nonstick skillet over medium-high heat. Add the mustard seeds. When they start popping, add the ginger, green chiles, and onion. Sauté for a few minutes until the onions turn golden brown. Add the fenugreek leaves, chile powder, asafetida, turmeric, and salt; sauté for 3 to 4 minutes. Remove from the heat. ❊ In a medium saucepan, combine the masoor dal, water, turmeric, and salt to taste; bring to a boil. Boil until lentils are just tender (about 10 minutes). Drain the dal. ❊ Add the dal and lemon juice to the fenugreek mixture. Mix well. Cook for a few minutes over low heat until the dal is totally dry. ❊ Serve hot, garnished with julienned ginger. ❊ VARIATIONS: Try this dish with whole moong dal for a more robust flavor.

EACH SERVING PROVIDES: CALORIES: 92; PROTEIN: 4 G; CARBOHYDRATES: 12 G; FAT: 3 G

WEB BITES | Check out Kate's Global Kitchen for more hints on cooking dals:
http://www.globalgourmet.com/food/kgk/2000/0300/tips.html

baked cauliflower with tender peas (dum gobhi)*

Prep Time: 20 minutes
Cooking Time: 45 minutes

. . . .

1 medium cauliflower, main stem removed	2 small tomatoes, chopped
1 tablespoon / 15 mL vegetable oil	1 cup / 250 mL fresh or frozen peas
1 small onion, chopped	½ cup / 125 mL water
1 tablespoon / 15 mL ginger garlic paste	2 teaspoons / 10 mL turmeric
1 tablespoon / 15 mL finely chopped fresh coriander	1 teaspoon / 5 mL red chile powder
	1 teaspoon / 5 mL garam masala
1 green chile, finely chopped	Salt to taste

STEAM whole head of cauliflower for 30 minutes. Drain and place in a medium casserole dish. ✲ Meanwhile, preheat oven to 375°F / 190°C. ✲ Heat the oil in a nonstick skillet. Add the onion; sauté until golden brown. Add the ginger garlic paste, coriander, and green chile; sauté for 2 minutes. Add the tomatoes; cook until the oil bubbles on the sides of the masala. ✲ Stir in the peas, water, turmeric, chile powder, garam masala, and salt. Cover and cook until the peas are done (6 to 8 minutes). ✲ Spread the peas masala over the cauliflower. Bake, uncovered, for 15 minutes or until the top starts to brown. ✲ VARIATIONS: Sprinkle some grated paneer on top of the cauliflower just before baking.
EACH SERVING PROVIDES: CALORIES: 83; PROTEIN: 4 G; CARBOHYDRATES: 10 G; FAT: 3 G

Cauliflower absorbs spices really well. For this recipe, select a compact cauliflower.

Tips: Bake this dish in the same bowl that you intend to serve it in.

To keep cauliflower snowy white as it steams, add 2 tablespoons / 25 mL lemon juice or white vinegar to the cooking water.

fiery pork (pork vindaloo)***

Prep Time: 20 minutes, plus 1 hour for marinating
Cooking Time: 35 minutes

. . . .

1 pound / 500 g pork, cubed

FOR THE MARINADE:

6 cloves garlic	¼ cup / 60 mL rice vinegar
1 inch / 2.5 cm peeled ginger	1 teaspoon / 5 mL peppercorns
2 green chiles	

FOR THE CHILE PASTE:

2 whole dried red chiles	1 teaspoon / 5 mL cumin seeds
4 (1-inch / 2.5-cm) pieces of cinnamon stick	¼ cup / 60 mL rice vinegar

The word "vindaloo" comes from the Portuguese words for vinegar and garlic. This dish is native to the Indian state of Goa and is known for its fiery hot taste.

Salt tends to toughen meat, so always add it at the end of cooking.

CONTINUED . . .

Tips: This dish tastes better the next day, after the flavors have had a chance to penetrate the meat.

2 tablespoons / 25 mL vegetable oil
½ cup / 125 mL onions, chopped
1 cup / 250 mL water

1 teaspoon / 5 mL sugar
Salt to taste

To make the marinade, in a blender or food processor, grind together the garlic, ginger, chiles, vinegar, and peppercorns to make a paste. Add the pork, turning to coat, and marinate, covered and refrigerated, for at least 1 hour. ❈ Meanwhile, make the chile paste. In the cleaned blender or food processor, grind together the red chiles, cinnamon sticks, cumin seeds, and vinegar. Set aside. ❈ In a large skillet, heat the oil over medium-high heat. Add the onions; sauté until golden brown. Stir in the chile paste. Cook, stirring constantly, until the oil rises to the surface (about 4 minutes). ❈ Add the marinated meat and sauté until all the liquid evaporates and the meat turns deep brown. Add the water, reduce the heat to low, and cook until the meat is tender (10 to 15 minutes). Stir in the sugar and salt. Serve immediately. ❈ VARIATIONS: You can add a tablespoon of brandy at the end. In Goa, where this dish originates, a tablespoon of feni (cashew nut wine) is often added at the end.

EACH SERVING PROVIDES: CALORIES: 180; PROTEIN: 17 G; CARBOHYDRATES: 5 G; FAT: 9 G

indian coleslaw

Prep Time: 20 minutes
Cooking Time: None

1 cucumber, finely diced
1 red onion, finely diced
1 tablespoon / 15 mL fresh coriander
  leaves, finely chopped
1 small tomato, finely diced

1 green chile, finely chopped
Juice of 1 lemon
1 tablespoon / 15 mL finely ground peanuts
¼ teaspoon / 1 mL red chile powder
Salt to taste

In a bowl combine the cucumber, onion, coriander, tomato, chile, lemon juice, peanuts, chile powder, and salt. Toss well. Serve. ❈ VARIATIONS: A good friend of mine who is from South India has a wonderfully cooling variation on this salad. She omits the peanuts and adds 2 tablespoons / 25 mL whipped low-fat plain yogurt and a tadka of mustard seeds and curry leaves (see page 15).

EACH SERVING PROVIDES: CALORIES: 24; PROTEIN: 1 G; CARBOHYDRATES: 2 G; FAT: 1 G

An American friend of mine was trying to get her son to eat this salad I'd just created. "What is it?" he asked. Her innovative reply was, "Indian Coleslaw." It worked like a charm. He had his salad, and I got a great name for my recipe.

oven-baked indian bread
(tandoori paratha)

Prep Time: 20 minutes
Cooking Time: 35 minutes

. . . .

1 ½ cups / 375 mL whole wheat flour
1 ½ cups / 375 mL all-purpose flour
1 ½ teaspoons / 7 mL salt

1 cup / 250 mL warm water
4 tablespoons / 60 mL melted butter
1 teaspoon / 5 mL fennel seeds, crushed

SIEVE the whole wheat flour, all-purpose flour, and salt into a mixing bowl. Add the water and knead the dough with your hands until it is fairly smooth but still a bit sticky. Cover with plastic wrap and set aside for 20 minutes. ❋ Add 1 tablespoon / 15 mL of the butter to the dough and knead until soft and smooth. Add the fennel seeds. Knead for another 3 or 4 minutes or until the dough is smooth and no longer sticky. ❋ Divide the dough into 12 equal portions. Roll each into a ball. On a lightly floured work surface, roll each ball into a very thin, crêpe-like 10-inch / 25-cm circle. Lightly spread some butter over each round. ❋ Using a sharp knife, make a cut from the center of each round to its outer edge and roll into a cone. Flatten each cone between your palms. On a lightly floured work surface, gently roll out the dough into 8-inch / 20-cm circles but not as thin as before; do not press too hard. ❋ Preheat the broiler. Lightly grease a cookie sheet. ❋ Place the dough rounds on the cookie sheet. Sprinkle with a few drops of water. Broil on the top rack until the bread is golden brown and black spots have appeared (about 4 minutes). Flip the parathas and cook on the other side until golden brown and some black spots appear. ❋ Serve immediately, or wrap in foil and reheat in a 300°F / 150°C oven until warmed through. ❋ VARIATIONS: Many people use milk along with the water to make the dough softer. This will gives the paratha a richer texture and creamier flavor. Also, you can cook this bread in a skillet. ❋ MAKES: 12

EACH SERVING PROVIDES: CALORIES: 251; PROTEIN: 7 G; CARBOHYDRATES: 45 G; FAT: 5 G

To give you an idea of how much this bread is part of the Indian culture and history, there is a street in Old Delhi named Paranthewali Gali, or the Paratha Lane, where some vendors have been selling parathas for the past 150 years.

Tips: When rolling out the dough for the second time, do not press down on the rounds too hard. Doing so will take away from the characteristic flakiness of this bread.

When this dish was served at a dinner I attended, no one around the table could tell what the crunchy "things" were in the yogurt. The chef finally obliged — rice. We could not have guessed it in a million years.

Tips: Leftover rice works best for this recipe. Bring the rice to room temperature before frying.

For a healthier version, try any grated cooked vegetable of your choice.

whipped yogurt sauce with rice pearls (raita)

Prep Time: 20 minutes
Cooking Time: 5 minutes

2 cups / 500 mL vegetable oil
2 tablespoons / 25 mL cooked white rice
1 cup / 250 mL fat-free plain yogurt, whipped
1 cup / 250 mL water

1 teaspoon / 5 mL roasted cumin seeds
1 teaspoon / 5 mL red chile powder
1 teaspoon / 5 mL salt
1 teaspoon / 5 mL sugar
Garnish: Finely chopped fresh coriander

HEAT the oil in a medium saucepan over medium-high heat. Add the rice. Fry until the rice is crisp (about 3 minutes). Drain the rice on paper towels. Let cool. ❋ In a mixing bowl combine the rice, yogurt, water, cumin seeds, chile powder, salt, and sugar. Garnish with coriander. Serve immediately. ❋ VARIATIONS: Deep-fried grated potatoes add a nice crunch to this dish.
EACH SERVING PROVIDES: CALORIES: 110; PROTEIN: 3 G; CARBOHYDRATES: 10 G; FAT: 8 G

The joy of this scrumptious dish is that it's so simple.

Tips: The quality of this dessert depends on how well the mixture is whisked together. You can use an electric mixer or a food processor to get a really smooth mix.

sweetened yogurt with saffron (shrikhand)

Prep Time: 20 minutes, plus 6 hours for chilling
Cooking Time: 10 minutes

½ teaspoon / 2 mL saffron
2 tablespoons / 25 mL warm milk
2 cups / 500 mL hung fat-free plain yogurt (page 20)

2 tablespoons / 25 mL sugar
½ teaspoon / 2 mL ground cardamom
Garnish: Slivered almonds

IN a large bowl, soak the saffron in warm milk for 10 minutes. Whisk in the yogurt, sugar, and cardamom until smooth and creamy. Cover and chill for at least 6 hours. Serve garnished with almonds. ❋ VARIATIONS: Add 1 cup / 250 mL of sweetened mango pulp (available in cans at Indian grocery stores) for a delightful saffron mango Indian mousse.
EACH SERVING PROVIDES: CALORIES: 90; PROTEIN: 5 G; CARBOHYDRATES: 12 G; FAT: 4 G

indian bread stuffed with cauliflower
(parathas)

. . . .

MASH any remaining Baked Cauliflower. Make and roll out the dough for the Oven-Baked Indian Bread. Place about a tablespoon / 15 mL of the mashed cauliflower in the center. Pull the sides together, pinching them firmly to join at the center. Roll out on a lightly floured work surface; do not press too hard with the rolling pin or the stuffing will break out.

Heat a medium skillet over medium heat. Add ¼ teaspoon / 1 mL of oil. When it is hot but not smoking, add the parathas. Cook until golden brown on each side. Serve with yogurt.

indian bread stuffed with dried lentils
(parathas)

. . . .

SAME method as above, but use leftover Stir-Fried Dried Lentils. Serve with yogurt.

Serves 4
—※—

FOR OUR FAMILY, SUNDAY
IS A DAY OF TOGETHERNESS.
When I was growing up we lived in
a joint family — uncles, aunts, and
grandparents all living under one roof. We
would all sit down to brunch on Sunday and
there would be talk about everything under the
sun: new girlfriends, bad bosses, the nasty traffic.
It was a time of sharing, and not just of food.
The joint family system has given way to
the nuclear family now, and traditions
are changing. But I would like to
keep Sunday brunch alive.
. . . .

◈ = EXPRESS MENU

hearty sunday brunch

Make this drink a Sunday-morning tradition in your home.

Tips: This drink has a shelf life of a few hours. Keep it refrigerated, and stir well before serving.

Try the Russian way of serving these eggs. Instead of slicing the eggs lengthwise, cut the top off and remove the yolk. Place the filled eggs upside down on a serving plate, cover with the tops, and sprinkle with cayenne pepper. Your "Spicy White Mushrooms" are ready to be served.

My cousin Dimple taught me how to make this. She is by far one of the best non-vegetarian cooks I know. Her husband is a sworn vegetarian, so I keep teasing him that he doesn't know what he's missing.

sweet buttermilk

Preparation Time: 5 minutes
Cooking Time: None

1 ½ cups / 375 mL fat-free plain yogurt
1 tablespoon / 15 mL sugar

1 tablespoon / 15 mL honey
5 or 6 ice cubes

PUT the yogurt, sugar, honey, and ice in a blender; blend until smooth. Serve chilled.
✳ VARIATIONS: You can replace the honey with a few drops of rose water.
EACH SERVING PROVIDES: CALORIES: 55; PROTEIN: 2 G; CARBOHYDRATES: 7 G; FAT: 0 G

spicy devils**

Prep Time: 25 minutes
Cooking Time: 5 minutes

4 hard-boiled eggs
1 tablespoon / 15 mL finely chopped
   fresh coriander
1 teaspoon / 5 mL toasted cumin seeds

1 teaspoon / 5 mL red chile powder
1 teaspoon / 5 mL red chile sauce (optional)
Salt to taste

WHILE the eggs are still warm, halve them lengthwise and carefully scoop out the yolks. Place the yolks in a mixing bowl and mash with a fork. Add the coriander, cumin, chile powder, chile sauce, and salt; stir together well. Spoon the mixture into the egg whites. Serve warm. ✳ VARIATIONS: You can add a tablespoon of fat-free mayonnaise to the mixture instead of the red chile sauce. Add a dash of Tabasco to liven up this dish.
EACH SERVING PROVIDES: CALORIES: 70; PROTEIN: 5 G; CARBOHYDRATES: 0 G; FAT: 5 G

dry chile chicken****

Prep Time: 5 minutes, plus 1 hour for marinating
Cooking Time: 45 minutes

1 pound / 500 g skinless, boneless chicken,
   cut into 1-inch / 2.5-cm strips
4 to 5 green chiles, seeded and chopped
¼ cup / 60 mL vinegar
1 tablespoon / 15 mL vegetable oil
2 teaspoons / 10 mL mustard seeds
8 cloves garlic, crushed
1 tablespoon / 15 mL ginger garlic paste

Leaves from 8 to 10 sprigs of curry
1 teaspoon / 5 mL red chile powder
1 teaspoon / 5 mL garam masala
1 teaspoon / 5 mL turmeric
Salt to taste
¼ cup / 60 mL water
Garnish: Ground coriander

In a mixing bowl, stir together the chicken, green chiles, and vinegar. Marinate, covered and refrigerated, for 1 hour. ✳ Heat the oil in a large skillet over medium-high heat. Add the mustard seeds. When the seeds crackle, add the garlic and chicken with its marinade. Sauté for 3 to 4 minutes to brown the chicken. Add the ginger garlic paste and the curry leaves. Sauté for another 2 to 3 minutes. ✳ Add the chile powder, garam masala, turmeric, and salt. Mix well. Stir in the water. Reduce heat to medium-low, cover, and cook until the chicken is tender (about 20 minutes). Remove the cover, reduce the heat to low, and simmer until the water dries up. ✳ Sprinkle with coriander and serve hot. ✳ VARIATIONS: Use chicken drumsticks (with bone). This dish is not for the faint-hearted: vary the chile according to your taste.

EACH SERVING PROVIDES: CALORIES: 182; PROTEIN: 32 G; CARBOHYDRATES: 2 G; FAT: 5 G

baby browns: chickpeas in black pepper sauce (chole)**

Prep Time: 25 minutes
Cooking Time: 35 minutes

2 small onions
2 (14-ounce / 398-mL) cans chickpeas, rinsed and drained
3 cups / 750 mL water
8 cloves garlic, peeled
2 whole cloves
1 cinnamon stick
2 to 3 black cardamom pods
1 teaspoon / 5 mL carom seeds (ajwain)
1 teaspoon / 5 mL salt
2 tablespoons / 25 mL vegetable oil

1 inch / 2.5 cm peeled ginger, shredded
3 tomatoes, chopped
1 teaspoon / 5 mL red chile powder
1 teaspoon / 5 mL mango powder
1 teaspoon / 5 mL roasted cumin seeds
1 tablespoon / 15 mL tamarind paste, dissolved in ¼ cup / 60 mL warm water
½ teaspoon / 2 mL garam masala
Garnish: Shredded ginger, finely chopped coriander, and 1 finely chopped small onion

SLICE 1 onion; set aside. Chop remaining onion. ✳ In a medium saucepan combine the chopped onion, chickpeas, water, garlic, whole cloves, cinnamon, cardamom, carom seeds, and salt. Bring to a boil; boil for 15 minutes. Set aside. ✳ In a large skillet over medium-high heat, heat the oil. Sauté the sliced onions until golden. Stir in the ginger and tomatoes. Sauté until the tomatoes are soft and the oil separates from the mixture. Add the chile powder, mango powder, and cumin seeds. Sauté for another 5 minutes. ✳ Stir in the chickpea mixture, tamarind paste, and ¼ teaspoon / 1 mL of the garam masala. Cook until most of the liquid has been absorbed. Discard the cinnamon stick. ✳ Serve hot, garnished

CONTINUED . . .

Tips: This dish tastes best with leg meat, so buy thighs or drumsticks.

These chickpeas are a Delhi favorite. Traditionally, they are eaten with bhature, a deep-fried bread. I love to eat them with plain white bread or lightly toasted pitas.

Tips: If you use dried chickpeas, soak them overnight first. When you boil them, add a pinch of baking soda to make them cook faster.

Many Indian grocery stores sell a masala known as chana masala. Add a teaspoon along with the mango powder to give an even more authentic taste.

with remaining ¼ teaspoon / I mL garam masala, ginger, coriander, and onion.
✳ VARIATIONS: Instead of the tamarind paste, you can use I cup / 250 mL of tea made with black tea leaves.
EACH SERVING PROVIDES: CALORIES: 3 I 3; PROTEIN: I 2 G; CARBOHYDRATES: 42 G; FAT: I I G

WEB BITES | Here is a very interesting article on cooking all types of beans: http://www.townonline.com/cambridge/entertainment/cooking/029781_2_how_021897_2bfaf95f00.html

spinach and corn bake

Prep Time: 25 minutes
Cooking Time: 35 minutes

2 tablespoons / 25 mL butter
2 tablespoons / 25 mL all-purpose flour
I cup / 250 mL I% milk
Salt and pepper to taste
I pound / 500 g fresh spinach, blanched
I tablespoon / I 5 mL vegetable oil
I small onion, chopped
I green chile, finely chopped
2 to 3 cloves garlic, crushed

I small tomato, chopped
I teaspoon / 5 mL grated ginger
I red bell pepper, chopped
½ cup / I 25 mL grated paneer
I tablespoon / I 5 mL chopped
    fresh coriander
I (I 4-ounce / 398-mL) can creamed corn
Garnish: Thinly sliced tomato, grated
    paneer, and shredded green chile

IN a medium nonstick saucepan over low heat, melt the butter. Add the flour; cook for 2 minutes, stirring constantly. Remove from the heat; slowly add the milk, stirring constantly until well blended. Return to the heat and cook for 2 to 3 minutes, stirring constantly, or until the sauce thickens. Remove from the heat. Stir in salt and pepper. ✳ Add the spinach and mix well until the spinach is well coated. Set aside. ✳ In a large nonstick skillet over medium heat, heat the oil. Add the onion; sauté until golden brown. Add the green chile, garlic, tomato, and ginger. Sauté until the tomato is soft. Add the red pepper, paneer, and salt to taste. Sauté for another 3 to 4 minutes or until the red pepper is cooked through. ✳ Preheat the broiler. Lightly grease a large casserole dish. ✳ Spread the spinach in the casserole dish. Add a layer of the paneer mixture. Sprinkle with half of the coriander. Repeat the layers. Top with the creamed corn. Garnish with the tomato, grated paneer, and green chile. ✳ Broil until the paneer is golden brown. Serve immediately. ✳ VARIATIONS: Instead of the corn, add a layer of thinly sliced cooked eggplant. You can also add a layer of thinly sliced cooked potatoes.
EACH SERVING PROVIDES: CALORIES: 220; PROTEIN: 8 G; CARBOHYDRATES: I 2 G; FAT: I 4 G

Although this is not a traditional Indian dish, over the years it has become a family favorite.

Tips: I often use a small transparent casserole to show off the brilliant colors of the layers in this dish.

potatoes and tomatoes in coriander ginger sauce (aloo tariwale)*

Prep Time: 15 minutes
Cooking Time: 35 minutes

2 tablespoons / 25 mL vegetable oil
¼ cup / 60 mL chopped fresh coriander
2 tablespoons / 25 mL grated ginger
1 teaspoon / 5 mL cumin seeds
3 whole green chiles, split lengthwise
3 tomatoes, chopped

1 teaspoon / 5 mL red chile powder
½ teaspoon / 2 mL turmeric powder
Salt to taste
5 potatoes, peeled and diced
1 cup / 250 mL water
Garnish: Pinch of dried fenugreek

In a large skillet over medium heat, heat the oil until it smokes. Add the coriander, ginger, and cumin seeds. Sauté for 30 seconds. Add the green chiles and tomatoes; sauté until the tomatoes are soft. Add the chile powder, turmeric, and salt. Mix well. ✳ Stir in the potatoes. Sauté for 2 minutes. Add the water. Bring to a boil, lower the heat, and simmer, covered, until the potatoes are tender (about 25 minutes). ✳ Serve garnished with the fenugreek. ✳ VARIATIONS: You can use whole tiny new potatoes in their jackets. Scrub them well to remove any dirt.

EACH SERVING PROVIDES: CALORIES: 180; PROTEIN: 4 G; CARBOHYDRATES: 32 G; FAT: 4 G

WEB BITES | Remember Mr. Potato Head? This site has nothing to do with potatoes; it is a fun site for fans of Mr. Edible Starchy Tuber Head:
http://winnie.acsu.buffalo.edu/potatoe/

To experience this dish at its best, use fresh tomatoes.

Tips: If you use whole new potatoes, prick them all over with a fork to ensure that the spices have an opening to sink into.

stir-fried chile lamb**

Prep Time: 15 minutes
Cooking Time: 45 minutes

1 pound / 500 g lean lamb, trimmed
    of fat and cubed
3 to 4 green chiles, halved lengthwise
    and seeded
½ cup / 125 mL chopped fresh coriander
2 tablespoons / 25 mL white vinegar
1 tablespoon / 15 mL ginger garlic paste

½ teaspoon / 2 mL red chile powder
¼ teaspoon / 1 mL turmeric
¼ teaspoon / 1 mL garam masala
¼ teaspoon / 1 mL ground coriander
Salt to taste
½ cup / 125 mL water

FOR THE GARNISH:

1 tablespoon / 15 mL vegetable oil
1 large onion, thinly sliced
Leaves from 2 sprigs of curry

Pinch of chaat masala
Pinch of ground coriander

This is one dish that rarely has any leftovers. Try it for yourself to see why.

Tips: I use the leg and shoulder cuts for this recipe. Australian lamb is by far the best that I have had.

CONTINUED . . .

In a mixing bowl combine the lamb, chiles, fresh coriander, vinegar, ginger garlic paste, chile powder, turmeric, garam masala, ground coriander, and salt. ✳ Heat a large saucepan over medium heat. Add the lamb mixture and the water. Cover and cook for 15 minutes, stirring occasionally, until the lamb starts to get tender. Remove the cover and increase the heat to high. Sauté until the lamb is fully cooked and tender, about 15 minutes. Add a little water if necessary to keep the lamb from sticking to the pan. Remove from the heat and keep warm. ✳ To make the garnish, in a large skillet over medium-high heat, heat the oil. Add the onion; sauté for 1 minute or until the onion is softened. Add the curry leaves. Cook for another 2 to 3 minutes or until the onions are golden brown. ✳ Place the sautéed lamb in the center of a serving platter. Create a ring around the lamb with the onion and curry leaves mixture. Sprinkle with chaat masala and ground coriander. Serve hot. ✳ VARIATIONS: I have substituted chicken or beef many times. Personally, I find that this recipe tastes the best with lamb.

EACH SERVING PROVIDES: CALORIES: 158; PROTEIN: 18 G; CARBOHYDRATES: 6 G; FAT: 9 G

WEB BITES | This site has some good information on selecting cuts of lamb:
http://www.woolgrowers.org/WoolAssociation/index2/links/recipes/lambcook.html

spicy indian bread (parathas)*

Prep Time: 35 minutes
Cooking Time: 25 minutes

2 cups / 500 mL whole wheat flour
2 cups / 500 mL all-purpose flour
Salt to taste
1 onion, finely chopped

1-inch / 2.5-cm piece peeled ginger, finely grated
1 green chile, finely chopped
3 tablespoons / 45 mL oil
1 ½ cups / 375 mL (approx.) hot water

SIEVE the whole wheat flour, all-purpose flour, and salt into a bowl. Stir in the onion, ginger, and green chile. Stir in 1 tablespoon / 15 mL of the oil. Add the water while kneading into a dough. Knead until the dough is smooth, about 10 minutes. Cover the dough with plastic wrap and set aside for 30 minutes. ✳ Divide the dough into 12 portions. Roll each into a ball. On a lightly floured surface, roll each ball into a thin circle about 10 inches / 25 cm in diameter. Brush a little oil over each round. ✳ Heat a medium skillet over medium-high heat. When it is hot, place a round of dough in it and dry roast until brown speaks appear on the underside. Turn the bread. Brush a little oil over the surface and drizzle a little oil around the bread. Cook until both sides are golden brown. Drain the paratha on paper towels. Repeat with the remaining dough. ✳ Serve immediately, or wrap in foil and reheat in a 300°F / 150°C oven until warmed through. ✳ VARIATIONS: Add dried fenugreek or finely chopped cooked spinach along with the onions. ✳ MAKES: 12

EACH SERVING PROVIDES: CALORIES: 260; PROTEIN: 8 G; CARBOHYDRATES: 48 G; FAT: 5 G

Try this bread on its own one evening; with a side of yogurt, you have a complete meal.

Tips: Make sure you finely chop the onion, or the pieces will break away from the bread.

This bread freezes well.

bird's nest salad

Prep Time: 15 minutes
Cooking Time: 10 minutes

. . . .

1 clove garlic, minced

1 jalapeño or green chile, minced

3 tablespoons / 45 mL lemon juice

2 tablespoons / 25 mL chopped
    fresh coriander

¼ teaspoon / 1 mL ground cumin

Salt and freshly ground black pepper to taste

1 red onion, sliced

1 cup / 250 mL canned chickpeas,
    drained and rinsed

1 cup / 250 mL canned red kidney beans,
    drained and rinsed

1 cup / 250 mL corn kernels, drained
    and rinsed

¼ cup / 60 mL bean sprouts

¼ cup / 60 mL diced red bell pepper

¼ teaspoon / 1 mL red chile powder

1 bunch lettuce leaves of your choice

IN a large bowl whisk together the garlic, jalapeño, lemon juice, coriander, cumin, salt, and black pepper. Add the onion, chickpeas, kidney beans, corn, bean sprouts, bell pepper, and chile powder. Mix well. ✳ Arrange the lettuce leaves along the walls of a large glass bowl to form a bird's nest. Gently spoon the salad mixture into the bird's nest, being careful not to disturb the lettuce. Serve at room temperature. ✳ VARIATIONS: Add ¼ cup / 60 mL fresh pomegranate seeds or ¼ cup / 60 mL mandarin orange sections for wonderful flavor and delightful color.

EACH SERVING PROVIDES: CALORIES: 180; PROTEIN: 8 G; CARBOHYDRATES: 32 G; FAT: 2 G

This is a perfect side to any sandwich on a hot summer afternoon.

Tips: If you can't find fresh coriander, use fresh parsley instead. Dried coriander is not a substitute.

If you do not like the idea of using raw sprouts, boil them for a few minutes and then add to the salad.

pumpkin with whipped yogurt sauce

Prep Time: 20 minutes, plus 1 hour for chilling
Cooking Time: 5 minutes

. . . .

1 cup / 250 mL grated pumpkin
    (bottlegourd)

1 cup / 250 mL fat-free plain yogurt,
    whipped

1 cup / 250 mL water

1 teaspoon / 5 mL roasted cumin seeds

1 teaspoon / 5 mL red chile powder

1 teaspoon / 5 mL salt

1 teaspoon / 5 mL sugar

Garnish: Finely chopped fresh coriander

BOIL the pumpkin until tender. Drain. In a mixing bowl combine the pumpkin, yogurt, water, cumin seeds, chile powder, salt, and sugar. Chill for 1 hour. Serve garnished with coriander. ✳ VARIATIONS: Instead of white pumpkin, you can use fresh pomegranate seeds or diced pineapple. You do not need to cook the pomegranate or pineapple.

EACH SERVING PROVIDES: CALORIES: 35; PROTEIN: 2 G; CARBOHYDRATES: 6 G; FAT: TRACE

Bottlegourd, or white pumpkin, is a summer vegetable and has very high water content. A versatile vegetable, it is used in everything from yogurt sauces to lentils to desserts. Look for it in Indian grocery stores.

Rice pudding plays an important role in Indian cuisine. It is believed that rice pudding was the last meal the Lord Buddha had before his enlightenment. In North India it is served at the most auspicious occasions.

Tips: Aluminum foil is NOT a substitute for silver leaf, or varak. Varak is pure and edible silver foil. Ask your Indian grocer for it.

rice pudding (kheer)

Prep Time: 20 minutes
Cooking Time: 1 hour

½ cup / 125 mL basmati rice, washed and drained

2 cups / 500 mL 1% milk

1 (14-ounce / 398-mL) can fat-free evaporated milk

2 to 3 cardamom pods, bruised

Pinch of saffron threads, soaked in 1 tablespoon / 15 mL warm milk

¼ cup / 60 mL low-fat sweetened condensed milk

Garnish: A few blanched slivered almonds and silver leaf (optional)

COMBINE the rice, 1% milk, and evaporated milk in a heavy nonstick saucepan; bring to a boil. Add the cardamom. Lower heat and simmer, stirring frequently, until the rice is cooked and the grains are starting to break up (about 20 minutes). Add the saffron and condensed milk; simmer for another 7 minutes or until pudding is desired consistency. ✳ Place in a serving dish and garnish with the almonds and silver leaf. Serve warm or chilled. ✳ VARIATIONS: Try crushed unsalted pistachios as a garnish.
EACH SERVING PROVIDES: CALORIES: 223; PROTEIN: 9 G; CARBOHYDRATES: 34 G; FAT: 5 G

WEB BITES | This site, from Food TV, best explains the silver leaf, or varak:
http://www.foodtv.com/terms/tt-r2/0,1991,938,00.html

lamb and rice pilaf

THIS is a quick and dirty version of a fairly complicated dish (my apologies to gourmet cooks). Cook about a cup of rice. Heat the leftover lamb in a saucepan over medium heat. Add the rice; sauté for 2 minutes. Serve warm.

spinach-wich

LIGHTLY toast and butter 2 slices of bread. Spread some warmed leftover Spinach and Corn Bake on 1 slice. Cover with the other slice. Serve with tomato ketchup.

I GREW UP ON THE SMALL BUT GORGEOUS ISLAND OF BAHRAIN, in the Persian Gulf. The summers were hot, and the best way to cool off was to head to the beach. So each Friday — which is the day off in the Middle East — we would go to the beach with no-cook sandwiches, a huge pitcher or two of juice, and a big beach towel. Life was good.

. . . .

Serves 4
—❋—

bottoms up

getting started

where's the real food?

on the side

live a little

heavenly leftovers

◈ =EXPRESS MENU

a picnic basket
❋

I first tasted this refreshing drink at the Convent of St. Brigitta's in Bangalore, where the sisters would make us this thirst-quenching, cooling juice on hot summer days.

Tips: The flesh of the watermelon has a tendency to settle at the bottom of the glass. Stir well before serving.

watermelon juice

Prep Time: 15 minutes
Cooking Time: None

2 cups / 500 mL chopped
    seeded watermelon
1 cup / 250 mL crushed ice
2 teaspoons / 10 mL honey

¼ teaspoon / 1 mL freshly ground
    black pepper
Garnish: Fresh mint

IN a blender, combine the watermelon, crushed ice, honey, and black pepper; blend until smooth. Garnish with mint. Serve chilled. ✳ VARIATIONS: Some friends like to add 1 teaspoon / 5 mL of lemon juice to bring out the sweetness of the watermelon. Others don't necessarily like the tanginess the lemon adds.
EACH SERVING PROVIDES: CALORIES: 25 G; PROTEIN: TRACE; CARBOHYDRATES: 6 G; FAT: TRACE

Having grown up in the Persian Gulf, I developed a taste for hummus at a very young age. Hummus is an integral part of Arabic cuisine. I still remember an Arab friend often saying, "Wake up and smell the hummus!"

Tips: In the original version of this recipe, the skins are removed from the chickpeas. Although this is a time-consuming job, it does give the hummus a wonderful-ly smooth consistency.

hummus with pita slices

Prep Time: 5 minutes
Cooking Time: 10 minutes

2 cups / 500 mL canned chickpeas,
    rinsed and drained
½ cup / 125 mL tahini
½ cup / 125 mL lemon juice
¼ teaspoon / 1 mL garam masala

2 cloves garlic, crushed
Salt and pepper to taste
Garnish: Chopped fresh parsley and a pinch
    of red chile flakes
2 whole wheat pitas, cut into bite-sized pieces

IN a blender combine the chickpeas, tahini, lemon juice, garam masala, garlic, salt, and pepper; blend into a smooth paste. Transfer to a serving dish and garnish with parsley and chile flakes. Serve with pita slices. ✳ VARIATIONS: Hummus is originally a Middle Eastern dish; for a more authentic flavor, omit the garam masala and instead add a pinch each of ground cumin and ground coriander. You can also use this as a dip for raw vegetables.
✳ YIELD: About 2 cups/ 500 mL ✳ Serving size is 2 tablespoons / 25 mL.

EACH SERVING PROVIDES (HUMMUS ONLY): CALORIES: 86; PROTEIN: 4 G; CARBOHYDRATES: 10 G; FAT: 3 G

WEB BITES | All you ever wanted to know about hummus:
http://www.ritefoods.com/hummus.html

If you enjoyed the hummus, here is a link to other Mediterranean recipes:
http://www.paulawolfert.com/recipes.html
You can even get a starter kit to cook these recipes from www.ethnicgrocer.com

coriander chutney sandwiches*

Prep Time: 10 minutes
Cooking Time: 10 minutes

· ·

FOR THE CHUTNEY:

1 green chile

2 cloves garlic

3 cups / 750 mL packed fresh coriander

¼ cup / 60 mL unsweetened
desiccated coconut

1 tablespoon / 15 mL lemon juice

Salt to taste

FOR THE SANDWICHES:

8 slices bread

2 tablespoons / 25 mL light margarine or
butter substitute

1 seedless cucumber, thinly sliced

To make the chutney, in a blender combine the chile, garlic, coriander, coconut, lemon juice, and salt; blend until smooth. Add a tablespoon / 15 mL of water to get a thinner consistency, if desired. Transfer chutney to an airtight container. ✳ Remove the crust from the bread. For each sandwich, lightly butter 1 slice of bread. Spread 1 tablespoon / 15 mL of the chutney on the other slice. Place a few slices of cucumber on the buttered bread. Cover with the chutney-covered slice. Cut each sandwich in half diagonally and serve. ✳ VARIATIONS: Add thinly sliced tomatoes and a slice of your favorite cheese to the sandwich. ✳ YIELD: 4 sandwiches ✳ MAKES: about 2 cups /500 mL chutney. Serving size is 1 tablespoon / 15 mL.

EACH SERVING PROVIDES (PER SANDWICH): CALORIES: 160; PROTEIN: 4 G; CARBOHYDRATES: 24 G; FAT: 3 G

Chutney sandwiches were my favorite school lunch when I was growing up. This is my peanut butter and jelly substitute!

Tips: This chutney can be used as a dipping sauce with many Indian appetizers.

This chutney freezes well for 3 to 4 months. In the fridge it will keep for about a week. Ensure that you store it in an airtight container.

Don't throw away the bread crusts. Lightly toast them in a dry skillet. Let cool, then crumble; store in an airtight container. Use the crumbs to thicken gravies or soups.

I remember vividly, as a child whenever I had a tummy ache, my mother would give me some fresh mint leaves to chew on.

Tips: This chutney freezes well for 3 to 4 months. In the fridge it will keep for about a week. Ensure that you store it in an airtight container.

tangy mint chutney sandwiches*

Prep Time: 10 minutes
Cooking Time: 10 minutes

1 green chile
2 cups / 500 mL packed fresh mint
1 cup / 250 mL packed fresh coriander
1 tablespoon / 15 mL lemon juice

2 teaspoons / 10 mL tamarind paste, dissolved in 1 tablespoon / 15 mL warm water
Salt to taste

FOR THE SANDWICHES:
8 slices bread
2 tablespoons / 25 mL light margarine or butter substitute

In a blender, combine the chile, mint, coriander, lemon juice, tamarind paste, and salt; blend until smooth. Add a tablespoon / 15 mL of water to get a thinner consistency, if desired. Transfer chutney to an airtight container. ❄ Remove the crust from the bread. For each sandwich, lightly butter 1 slice of bread. Spread 1 tablespoon / 15 mL of the chutney on the other slice. Cover with the buttered slice. Cut each sandwich in half diagonally and serve. ❄ VARIATIONS: Two tablespoons / 25 mL of fat-free plain yogurt will give this chutney a much creamier taste. ❄ YIELD: 4 sandwiches ❄ MAKES: about 2 cups /500 mL chutney. Serving size is 1 tablespoon / 15 mL.

EACH SERVING PROVIDES (PER SANDWICH): CALORIES: 156; PROTEIN: 4 G; CARBOHYDRATES: 25 G; FAT: 3 G

WEB BITES | Check out this site for more on the medicinal power of mint: http://www.wahindia.com/wahbody/kitchen_med_pudina.asp

Spoon this chutney over steamed salmon for a savory and tangy dish. Or toss with your favorite pasta for a quick meal.

Tips: This chutney will keep for about a week in the fridge.

tomato chutney sandwiches

Prep Time: 10 minutes
Cooking Time: 10 minutes

1 tablespoon / 15 mL vegetable oil
1 teaspoon / 5 mL mustard seeds
Leaves from 1 sprig of curry
1 teaspoon / 5 mL crushed garlic
1 teaspoon / 5 mL crushed ginger
2 whole cloves

4 black peppercorns
1 green chile, minced
4 tomatoes, chopped
Salt to taste
2 tablespoons / 25 mL white vinegar
2 teaspoons / 10 mL sugar

FOR THE SANDWICHES:
8 slices bread
2 tablespoons / 25 mL light margarine or butter substitute

IN a large skillet over medium heat, heat the oil. Add the mustard seeds. When they begin to crackle, add the curry leaves, garlic, ginger, cloves, peppercorns, and green chile. Sauté for 30 seconds. Stir in the tomatoes. Cook for 10 minutes or until the tomatoes are soft. ❉ Reduce the heat to low, add the salt, and cook for 5 minutes. Stir in the vinegar and sugar; cook for another 2 to 3 minutes until all the flavors meld and you can smell the wonderful fragrance of the chutney. Let cool. Store in an airtight container. ❉ Remove the crust from the bread. For each sandwich, lightly butter 1 slice of the bread. Spread 1 tablespoon / 15 mL of the chutney on the other slice. Cover with the buttered slice. Cut each sandwich in half diagonally and serve. ❉ VARIATIONS: Instead of the garlic and ginger, add a teaspoon / 5 mL of tamarind paste for a tangier chutney. ❉ YIELD: 4 sandwiches ❉ MAKES: about 2 cups /500 mL chutney. Serving size is 1 tablespoon / 15 mL.

EACH SERVING PROVIDES (PER SANDWICH): CALORIES: 211; PROTEIN: 3 G; CARBOHYDRATES: 24 G; FAT: 3 G

curry leaves spice rub sandwiches

Prep Time: 5 minutes
Cooking Time: 20 minutes

30 to 35 curry leaves
2 tablespoons / 25 mL sesame seeds
2 tablespoons / 25 mL roasted peanuts
1 teaspoon / 5 mL mango powder

¼ teaspoon / 1 mL red chile powder
Pinch of sugar
Salt to taste

FOR THE SANDWICHES:
8 slices bread
2 tablespoons / 25 mL light margarine or butter substitute

PLACE the curry leaves in a large skillet and heat over medium-low heat. Dry roast the curry leaves, stirring frequently, for about 15 minutes, until the leaves are crisp and a wonderful black color. Let cool. ❉ In a blender, combine the curry leaves, sesame seeds, peanuts, mango powder, chile powder, sugar, and salt; grind to a fine powder. Store in an airtight container. ❉ Remove the crust from the bread. For each sandwich, lightly butter both slices of the bread. Sprinkle 1 teaspoon / 5 mL of the spice rub onto 1 buttered slice. Cover with the other buttered slice. Cut the sandwich in half diagonally and serve. ❉ VARIATIONS: This spice rub makes a great topping for any whipped yogurt sauce. It is also used as an accompaniment to any meal. ❉ YIELD: 4 sandwiches ❉ MAKES: about 1 cup / 250 mL spice rub. Serving size is 1 teaspoon / 5 mL.

EACH SERVING PROVIDES (PER SANDWICH): CALORIES: 191; PROTEIN: 4 G; CARBOHYDRATES: 23 G; FAT: 4 G

My mother-in-law submitted this recipe to a contest in Mumbai and won first prize. She competed with 80 other women.

Tips: Go ahead and increase the amount of spice rub in each sandwich if you enjoy stronger flavors.

The rub will keep for up to a month in the fridge.

This is my substitute for peanut butter. I like the powdered nature of this recipe. You can make it a paste if you keep grinding it.

Tips: This is a great substitute for salt on French fries!

peanut spice rub sandwiches

Prep Time: 5 minutes
Cooking Time: 10 minutes

1 teaspoon / 5 mL vegetable oil	¼ cup / 60 mL roasted peanuts
2 whole red chiles	½ teaspoon / 2 mL salt
Pinch of asafetida	½ teaspoon / 2 mL sugar
¼ cup / 60 mL roasted sesame seeds	¼ teaspoon / 1 mL mango powder

FOR THE SANDWICHES:
8 slices bread
2 tablespoons / 25 mL light margarine or butter substitute

IN a small skillet over medium-high heat, heat the oil. Sauté the red chiles and the asafetida for 30 seconds. In a coffee/spice mill, grind the chiles, asafetida, and sesame seeds to a fine powder. Crush the peanuts to a coarse powder. Add to the red chile mixture. Add the salt, sugar, and mango powder. Mix well. ❊ Remove the crust from the bread. For each sandwich, lightly butter both slices of the bread. Sprinkle about 1 teaspoon / 5 mL of the spice rub onto 1 slice. Cover with the other buttered slice. Cut the sandwich in half diagonally and serve. ❊ VARIATIONS: You can omit the red chiles if you find this rub too spicy. ❊ YIELD: 4 sandwiches ❊ MAKES: about 1 cup / 250 mL spice rub. Serving size is 1 teaspoon / 5 mL.

EACH SERVING PROVIDES (PER SANDWICH): CALORIES: 189: PROTEIN: 4 G; CARBOHYDRATES: 23 G; FAT: 4 G

I first prepared this for a friend's shower. The entire menu was Italian and tasted pretty mild. I needed something to kick it up a notch, and my mother provided this fun recipe. Look for chile garlic sauce at Indian grocery stores.

tri-colored pepper pasta

Prep Time: 20 minutes
Cooking Time: 35 minutes

8 ounces / 250 g tri-colored pasta shells	1 red bell pepper, julienned
2 tablespoons / 25 mL vegetable oil	1 green bell pepper, julienned
3 tomatoes, finely chopped	1 yellow bell pepper, julienned
2 whole cloves	1 green chile, finely chopped
3 cardamom pods	1 teaspoon / 5 mL chile garlic
Salt to taste	sauce (optional)
½ teaspoon / 2 mL sugar	Garnish: Finely chopped fresh coriander
1 green onion, finely chopped	

BOIL the pasta according to directions on the package. Drain and set aside. ❊ Heat 1 table-spoon / 15 mL of the oil in a nonstick skillet over medium heat. Add the tomatoes, cloves, and cardamom. Cook, stirring occasionally, until the tomatoes are soft (about 5 minutes). Stir in the salt and sugar. Reduce heat and simmer for 2 minutes. Remove from the heat and let cool. ✳ In a food processor, purée the tomato mixture. Set aside. ✳ Wipe out the skillet and in it heat the remaining 1 tablespoon / 15 mL oil over medium heat. Add the green onion, bell peppers, and green chile; sauté until the vegetables are tender (about 8 minutes). Stir in the chile garlic sauce. Remove from the heat. ✳ In a large serving bowl, toss together the pasta, tomato sauce, and vegetable mixture. ✳ Serve at room temperature, garnished with chopped coriander. ✳ VARIATIONS: Sauté some shrimp along with the vegetables. Add a few sun-dried tomatoes for a true East-meets-West flavor.

EACH SERVING PROVIDES: CALORIES: 300; PROTEIN: 8 G; CARBOHYDRATES: 23 G; FAT: 8 G

mango cake

Prep Time: 40 minutes
Cooking Time: 35 minutes

· ·

1 cup / 250 mL semolina (sooji)
½ cup / 125 mL melted butter

3 cups / 750 mL sweetened mango pulp
1 teaspoon / 5 mL baking soda

IN a mixing bowl, stir together the semolina and melted butter. Set aside for 20 minutes. Add the mango pulp. Mix well. Set aside for another 20 minutes. ✳ Meanwhile, preheat the oven to 350°F / 180°C. Lightly grease a medium square baking dish. ✳ Stir the baking soda into the batter. Pour the batter into the baking dish and bake for 30 minutes or until a toothpick poked into the cake comes out clean. ✳ Let the cake cool in the pan, then turn it out onto a rack to cool completely. Slice and serve with a scoop of your favorite ice cream. ✳ VARIATIONS: Once when I ran out of mango pulp I used my baby's puréed pears. The cake was milder but still delicious. ✳ YIELD: 10 servings

EACH SERVING PROVIDES: CALORIES: 196; PROTEIN: 2 G; CARBOHYDRATES: 27 G; FAT: 8 G

WEB BITES | If you can't find canned mango pulp in Indian grocery stores, visit: www.namaste.com

Tips: Most grocery stores sell julienned bell peppers in frozen packets. These are great to have on hand when you're short on time.

This is my husband's favorite dessert. It is light and fluffy and has just the right amount of exotic mango flavor!

Tips: This cake will keep, refrigerated in an airtight container, for up to a week.

chutney fish

· ·

TRY this if you have any coriander and mint chutneys left over. In a bowl, stir together about 1 tablespoon / 15 mL of each chutney, 1 tablespoon / 15 mL of lemon juice, 1 tablespoon / 15 mL of ginger garlic paste, and salt to taste. Marinate 4 fish fillets of your choice (I recommend catfish) for about 20 minutes. In a large skillet over medium heat, heat 1 tablespoon / 15 mL of vegetable oil; sauté 1 finely chopped onion. When it is golden brown, add the fish. Lower the heat and add ½ cup / 125 mL of water. Simmer, covered, until the fish flakes easily with a fork (10 to 15 minutes). Serve with steamed white basmati rice.

I COOKED THIS MENU FOR MY HUSBAND on our first Valentine's Day together. I am living proof that the way to a man's heart is through his stomach — he proposed the next day. This is my hometown menu — my husband is from Bombay and I am from Delhi. ❄ Many of you may shake your head with intimidation when you see the Coconut Water in the drinks section. Trust me, you will enjoy it. It is naturally sweet and has a wonderful flavor that I have not found in anything else. ❄ In Asia many doctors recommend coconut water to patients who are dehydrated or recovering from surgery.

Serves 4

delhi fare for four

= EXPRESS MENU

I read somewhere that coconut water could be the next big thing in sports drinks for athletes. It's a natural isotonic beverage, containing the same level of electrolytic balance as we have in our blood. Don't confuse this drink with coconut milk: they are two entirely different things.

coconut water (nariyal pani)

Prep Time: 5 minutes
Cooking Time: None

4 tender green coconuts

USING a sharp knife, cut open the top of the coconut. Pour the coconut water into a tall glass. Chill. Add a few slices of the tender coconut to the water just before serving.

✻ VARIATIONS: It is only occasionally that I see tender green coconuts. You can buy coconut water in cans, ready to serve. Although the taste is not quite the same, it is a good substitute.

EACH SERVING PROVIDES: CALORIES: 48; PROTEIN: 3 G; CARBOHYDRATES: 9 G; FAT: TRACE

matching wines with indian food

WHETHER served before or with a meal, wine should complement the food and not overwhelm it, and vice versa. Strong curries will destroy the taste of light wines.

Here are some guidelines on matching wines with food.
Red meat: Heavy red wine
White meat: Full-bodied white wine
Fish/vegetables: Dry white wine/ Light red wine
Desserts: Sweet sherry

That is what the experts say. Here is what I say (did you expect anything less?):

✻ Drink what you like.

✻ In general, select full-bodied wines and heavy reds.

✻ Select wines that complement the food:
    Savory: Sparkling wines or fruity off-dry wines
    Creamy: Fruity red wines
    Grilled: Light red wines
    Spicy: Light-bodied wines (either color)

✻ Vinegar and lemon are natural enemies of wine. They will destroy the flavor of any wine.

steamed yellow spice cake (dhokla)**

Prep Time: 20 minutes, plus 6 hours to ferment
Cooking Time: 1 minute

. . . .

3 cups / 750 mL channa dal
1 teaspoon / 5 mL baking soda
¼ teaspoon / 1 mL turmeric
Salt to taste

FOR THE TADKA:
1 tablespoon / 15 mL vegetable oil
Leaves from 2 sprigs of curry

2 green chiles
1 tablespoon / 15 mL grated ginger
¼ teaspoon / 1 mL ENO Fruit Salt
    or baking powder

½ teaspoon / 2 mL mustard seeds
Pinch of asafetida

Garnish: Grated coconut, finely chopped
    fresh coriander, pinch of sugar, and
    pinch of red chile powder

SOAK the dal in enough water to cover for at least 4 hours. Drain the dal. In a blender, purée the dal. Add the soda, turmeric, and salt; mix well. Cover and set aside until the mixture ferments (at least 4 to 6 hours). ✳ In a blender, blend the green chile and ginger to a smooth paste. Stir into the fermented dal. Stir in the ENO. ✳ Lightly grease a medium plate. Spread about 1 cup / 250 mL of the batter on the plate (about 1 inch / 2.5 cm thick). Steam for 8 to 10 minutes or until the mixture is solid and firm (all the liquid has evaporated). Remove the cake from the plate and let cool on a rack. Repeat until all the batter is used. Cut cakes into a total of 12 bite-sized pieces and arrange on a serving plate. ✳ To prepare the tadka, heat the oil in a small saucepan over medium heat. Add the curry leaves, mustard seeds, and asafetida. When the mustard seeds begin to crackle, remove from the heat and pour over the steamed cakes. ✳ Garnish with the coconut, coriander, sugar, and chile powder and serve with Tamarind Chutney (page 84). ✳ VARIATIONS: Instead of the channa dal, use 2 cups / 500 mL of rice and 1 cup / 250 mL of urad dal. Dry roast the rice and dal in a hot skillet for about 5 minutes. In a blender, blend them to a fine paste. Add ¼ cup / 60 mL of plain yogurt and 1 cup / 250 mL of water to make a smooth batter. Let the batter ferment overnight. ✳ YIELD: 12 pieces

EACH SERVING PROVIDES (3 PIECES PER SERVING): CALORIES: 199; PROTEIN: 10 G; CARBOHYDRATES: 30 G; FAT: 4 G

I love using leaf-shaped cookie cutters to cut this cake. It makes an enticing presentation. These light, fluffy spice cakes are a perfect accompaniment to afternoon tea.

Tips: Any leftover cakes can be stored in the fridge for about 3 days.

Tamarind is a large evergreen tree that grows in the tropics. As a child, I would often climb tamarind trees and eat the delicious, tangy raw fruit.

Tips: The chutney will keep in the fridge, covered, for about a week.

tamarind chutney

Prep Time: 20 minutes
Cooking Time: 20 minutes

3 tablespoons / 45 mL tamarind pulp
1 cup / 250 mL hot water
3 tablespoons / 45 mL pitted and finely chopped dates
2 teaspoons / 10 mL brown sugar

½ teaspoon / 2 mL ground ginger
½ teaspoon / 2 mL ground coriander
¼ teaspoon / 1 mL red chile powder
Pinch of salt

IN a small saucepan, soak the tamarind pulp in the water for 10 minutes. Stir well to dissolve, and then stir in the dates. Simmer, covered, for 15 minutes. Let cool. ❋ Push the mixture through a sieve set over a bowl and discard the solids. Add the brown sugar, ginger, coriander, chile powder, and salt; mix well. ❋ Return the mixture to the saucepan and simmer for 5 to 10 minutes or until the sugar is completely dissolved. Let cool. ❋ Serve at room temperature with the Spice Cakes (page 83). ❋ VARIATIONS: A tablespoon / 15 mL of lemon juice will sharpen the flavor. ❋ YIELD: Makes about 1 cup / 250 mL. Serving size is 1 tablespoon / 15 mL.
EACH SERVING PROVIDES: CALORIES: 15; PROTEIN: TRACE; CARBOHYDRATES: 3 G; FAT: TRACE

WEB BITES

Did you know that tamarind is also an integral ingredient in Worcestershire sauce? Here's a site that tells you all you ever wanted to know about tamarind:
http://www.hort.purdue.edu/newcrop/morton/tamarind.html

This site features easy techniques on using dried tamarind bricks:
http://www2.alberta.com/food/columns/displayone.cfm?articleid=197

yogurt curry with
lentil dumplings (kadi)

Prep Time: 20 minutes
Cooking Time: 45 minutes

• •

Lentil Dumplings (page 32)
2 cups / 500 mL water
1 cup / 250 mL fat-free plain yogurt
2 tablespoons / 25 mL chickpea
    flour (besan)

¼ teaspoon / 1 mL turmeric
Salt to taste

FOR THE TADKA:
1 tablespoon / 15 mL vegetable oil
½ teaspoon / 2 mL mustard seeds
2 whole red chiles

Pinch of asafetida
Leaves from 2 sprigs of curry

COOK the dumplings, then soak in water and squeeze dry according to the recipe on page 32. Set aside. ✳ In a medium saucepan whisk together the water, yogurt, chickpea flour, turmeric, and salt. Simmer, stirring, over medium-low heat for 20 to 35 minutes or until the sauce begins to thicken to a custard-like consistency. Remove from the heat and add the dumplings. Pour into a serving dish and set aside. ✳ To prepare the tadka, heat the oil in a small saucepan over medium heat. Add the mustard seeds, red chiles, asafetida, and curry leaves. When the mustard seeds begin to crackle, remove from the heat and pour over the yogurt curry. ✳ Serve hot.

EACH SERVING PROVIDES: CALORIES: 334; PROTEIN: 17 G; CARBOHYDRATES: 39 G; FAT: 12 G

WEB BITES | This article on Indian cooking meeting the Western palate will make you smile: http://www.usnews.com/usnews/issue/990322/nycu/22indi.htm

I know, deep-fried dumplings, what was I thinking? But some traditions should live on. Kadi and rice has been a traditional holiday lunch at our house for the past five generations. There is more to this recipe than deep-fried dumplings.

Tips: Add a couple of cooked vegetables of your choice and this dish becomes a complete meal in itself. Serve with steamed white rice.

Asafetida is also known as stinking gum! It is a gum resin native to Iran and India. Don't worry about the unpleasant smell when it is raw; the odor disappears completely in cooking. This spice is legendary for its digestive properties.

Shallots are a gourmet member of the onion family. They are not used in traditional Indian cooking, but I like the mild flavor they impart to this dish. You can substitute red onions if you prefer.

Tips: Sambal is a hot and spicy chile sauce frequently used in Indonesian cooking. Look for it in Asian food stores or order it on the Internet (see the web bite at right).

shallot chicken and coconut curry*

Prep Time: 20 minutes
Cooking Time: 40 minutes

FOR THE SPICE PASTE:

1 tablespoon / 15 mL sambal	¼ teaspoon / 1 mL turmeric
½ teaspoon / 2 mL garam masala	¼ teaspoon / 1 mL chile powder
¼ teaspoon / 1 mL coriander powder	¼ teaspoon / 1 mL mango powder
¼ teaspoon / 1 mL cumin powder	

1 tablespoon / 15 mL vegetable oil	¼ cup / 60 mL curry leaves
1 tablespoon / 15 mL ginger garlic paste	Salt to taste
½ cup / 125 mL chopped shallots	½ pound / 250 g chicken thighs, skinned
(5 to 10 shallots)	½ cup / 125 mL light coconut milk
1 star anise	

To make the spice paste: In a small bowl combine the sambal, garam masala, coriander, cumin, turmeric, chile powder, and mango powder. Add water a few drops at a time to make a paste. Set aside. ✳ In a medium skillet over medium heat, heat the oil. Add the ginger garlic paste; sauté for 1 minute. Add the shallots; sauté for 3 minutes. Add the star anise and curry leaves. Sauté for another minute. Stir in the spice paste. Reduce heat to low and sauté for another 2 to 3 minutes. Add the salt. ✳ Increase heat to medium and add the chicken. Cook for 10 minutes. Add the coconut milk and simmer until the chicken is cooked through (about 20 minutes). ✳ VARIATIONS: You can add your choice of chicken pieces. Add a few peeled and diced turnips for a mellower flavor. Add a tablespoon / 15 mL of chile sauce to the curry instead of the sambal.

EACH SERVING PROVIDES: CALORIES: 165; PROTEIN: 13 G; CARBOHYDRATES: 12 G; FAT: 7 G

WEB BITES | You can order sambal from this site. Their Chile Garlic Sambal is particularly good. http://www.huyfong.com/no_frames/oelek.htm

baby eggplants with crushed onions (bagare baigan)*

Prep Time: 20 minutes
Cooking Time: 20 minutes

. . . .

6 small eggplants

4 teaspoons / 20 mL unsweetened
  desiccated coconut

4 teaspoons / 20 mL crushed peanuts

1 tablespoon / 15 mL chickpea flour

1 teaspoon / 5 mL coriander seeds

1 teaspoon / 5 mL cumin seeds

¼ teaspoon / 1 mL sesame seeds

¼ teaspoon / 1 mL fenugreek seeds

2 tablespoons / 25 mL vegetable oil

2 small onions, coarsely chopped

1 tablespoon / 15 mL ginger garlic paste

¼ cup / 60 mL curry leaves

¼ teaspoon / 1 mL turmeric

¼ teaspoon / 1 mL red chile powder

Salt to taste

1 tablespoon / 15 mL tamarind paste,
  dissolved in some warm water

RINSE the eggplant. Cut shallow slits along the sides of the eggplant. Do not cut through the stem. ✳ In a small skillet over medium heat, dry roast the coconut, peanuts, chickpea flour, coriander seeds, cumin seeds, sesame seeds, and fenugreek seeds for 1 minute or until fragrant. Let cool. In a coffee/spice mill, grind to a fine powder. ✳ In a large skillet over medium heat, heat the oil. Add the onion; sauté until golden brown. Add the ginger garlic paste and curry leaves; sauté for another 1 to 2 minutes. ✳ Stir in the dry spice powder, turmeric, chile powder, and salt. Stir well. Add the eggplants; sauté for 3 minutes. Add the tamarind paste. Simmer, covered, until the eggplant is tender (10 to 12 minutes). Add about ¼ cup / 60 mL water during the cooking if the curry is drying out. ✳ VARIATIONS: You can stuff the eggplant with the spice mixture instead of adding the spice mixture to the onions.
EACH SERVING PROVIDES: CALORIES: 175; PROTEIN: 5 G; CARBOHYDRATES: 15 G; FAT: 9 G

WEB BITES

Here is a site that has some good information on selecting raw vegetables and fruits (check out the eggplant section):
http://www.5aday.com/selection_tips.html

This site has an informative chart showing the shelf life of many fresh vegetables and fruits:
http://hgic.clemson.edu/factsheets/HGIC3483.htm

This recipe is special to me. Eggplant is my all-time favorite vegetable, but my husband would not have anything to do with it. No matter how I cooked it, he did not want to eat it. Then came this recipe, and now he is a true convert.

funky pink spice rice (gulabi chawal)

Prep Time: 20 minutes
Cooking Time: 20 minutes

1 tablespoon / 15 mL vegetable oil
¼ teaspoon / 1 mL mustard seeds
1 green chile, finely chopped
1 small onion, finely chopped
1 small eggplant, cubed
6 or 7 curry leaves

1 small beet, peeled, boiled, and diced
¼ teaspoon / 1 mL turmeric
Salt to taste
1½ cups / 375 mL cooked basmati rice
Garnish: Chopped fresh coriander

HEAT the oil in a nonstick skillet over medium heat. Add the mustard seeds and green chile. When the mustard seeds begin to crackle, add the onion. Sauté for 2 to 3 minutes or until the onions start to soften. Add the eggplant and curry leaves. Cook until the eggplant is soft (about 4 to 5 minutes). Add a tablespoon or two of water to prevent the spices from sticking to the pan, if necessary. ※ Stir in the beet; sauté for 2 to 3 minutes. Add the turmeric and salt; sauté for another 2 minutes. Stir in the rice. Cook, stirring occasionally, until the rice is heated through. ※ Serve hot, garnished with chopped coriander. ※ VARIATIONS: If you are not a big beet fan, substitute mussels for a whole different flavor!

EACH SERVING PROVIDES: CALORIES: 116; PROTEIN: 2 G; CARBOHYDRATES: 18 G; FAT: 4 G

mashed potato salad (aloo salad)

Prep Time: 20 minutes
Cooking Time: 5 minutes

1 large potato, boiled and peeled
1 cup / 250 mL fat-free plain yogurt
1 teaspoon / 5 mL roasted cumin seeds
¼ teaspoon / 1 mL finely chopped
　fresh coriander

Salt to taste
Sugar to taste

IN a medium bowl, coarsely mash the potato. Add the yogurt, cumin, coriander, salt, and sugar; stir well. Chill for about an hour. Serve. ※ VARIATIONS: For extra tang, add a dash of tamarind chutney (page 84).

EACH SERVING PROVIDES: CALORIES: 56; PROTEIN: 3 G; CARBOHYDRATES: 11 G; FAT: TRACE

Beets, I have to admit, are an acquired taste. They are wonderfully rich in vitamins and can be used in salads, soups, curries, yogurt sauces, and even for juices.

Tips: This dish tastes best with any white long-grain rice.

When I was single, this was a staple salad for me. I would keep a couple of boiled potatoes handy in the fridge to shorten the cooking time even further.

Tips: One of the easiest ways to cook potatoes is in the microwave. Simply prick the potatoes all over with a fork and microwave for about 15 minutes or until tender.

saffron fruit custard (kesari phal)

Prep Time: 10 minutes
Cooking Time: 10 minutes

¼ cup / 60 mL low-fat plain yogurt,
   whipped

3 tablespoons / 45 mL 1% milk

1 tablespoon / 15 mL sugar

Pinch of saffron, soaked in 2 tablespoons /
   25 mL warm milk

1 cup / 250 mL diced fresh fruit of
   your choice

IN a small bowl, blend the yogurt, milk, sugar, and saffron into a smooth sauce. Place the fruit in a serving bowl. Pour the saffron yogurt sauce over the fruit. Serve chilled.

❊ VARIATIONS: If you want a creamier sauce, use hung yogurt instead of regular yogurt (see page 20).

EACH SERVING PROVIDES: CALORIES: 50; PROTEIN: 1 G; CARBOHYDRATES: 12 G; FAT: TRACE

WEB BITES | When I started researching saffron, I was sure I would not find much information, since it's such a specialized ingredient. Boy, was I wrong. Here is "A contemporary guide to an ancient spice": http://www.saffroninfo.com

Another interesting site is http://www.herbsearch.com; go there to learn more about your favorite herb.

simple rice pilaf

TRY this recipe with any leftover shallot chicken. Reheat the chicken in a large skillet. Add about 1 cup / 250 mL of cooked basmati rice. Sauté on high heat for 2 to 3 minutes or until heated through. A simple rice pilaf! Serve with plain yogurt or yogurt with rice pearls (page 62).

My in-laws have been married for 37 years, and my mother-in-law makes this treat for my father-in-law on his birthday every year without fail.

Tips: As a rule of thumb, use about 3 threads of saffron per person.

Serves 2
—※—

an intimate dinner for two
(south indian)
※

I GAINED GREAT ADMIRATION AND RESPECT for South Indian food while I lived and went to college in the garden city of Southern India, Bangalore. The flavors were so different from those in my native North India. Everything was different: the culture, the people, the cuisine. I became a flavor explorer! I ate at every type of South Indian place, from the vendor on the street to the coffee shop of the five-star Taj Hotel. ※ Rice is a staple in the south and is cooked in many different ways. There is not a lot of focus on breads. The cuisine is delicious yet the sauces are simple to prepare.

· · · · · · · · · · · · ·

◈ = EXPRESS MENU

Rasam is known for its digestive powers. I often drink it after a heavy meal to ease heartburn.

spiced tomato juice (rasam)***

Prep Time: 10 minutes
Cooking Time: 10 minutes

3 tablespoons / 45 mL red gram dal
  (toor dal)
6 cups / 1.5 L water
4 tomatoes, finely chopped

1 green chile, finely chopped (optional)
1 teaspoon / 5 mL grated ginger
Salt to taste

FOR THE TADKA:
2 teaspoons / 10 mL vegetable oil
1 teaspoon / 5 mL mustard seeds
1 teaspoon / 5 mL cumin seeds

Pinch of asafetida
3 or 4 curry leaves

Garnish: Finely chopped fresh coriander

IN a medium saucepan, bring the dal and 3 cups / 750 mL of the water to a boil; boil until the dal is soft and creamy. Add the tomatoes, green chile, ginger, salt, and remaining 3 cups / 750 mL of water. Simmer until the tomatoes are soft and completely cooked (about 10 minutes). ❊ To prepare the tadka, heat the oil in a small saucepan over medium heat. Add the mustard seeds, cumin seeds, asafetida, and curry leaves. When the mustard seeds begin to crackle, remove from the heat and stir into the tomato juice. Simmer for another minute. ❊ Serve warm, garnished with coriander. ❊ VARIATIONS: If you like a tangier rasam, add about 2 teaspoons / 10 mL of tamarind paste to the dal when it is cooking.

EACH SERVING PROVIDES: CALORIES: 147; PROTEIN: 7 G; CARBOHYDRATES: 18 G; FAT: 6 G

WEB BITES | This wonderful site has 11 variations of rasam recipes:
http://www.indianrecipes.com/Soups/Rasam/

steamed stuffed semolina puffs (idlies)**

Prep Time: 20 minutes
Cooking Time: 25 minutes

. . . .

Steamed Semolina Savory Cakes (Idlies) (page 42)

1 tablespoon / 15 mL Indian mango pickle gravy

PREPARE a steamer and make the idli batter according to the recipe on page 42. After adding ENO to the batter, pour 3 tablespoons / 45 mL into each prepared bowl. Using your finger, make a well in the center of the cup. Drop about 3 to 4 drops of the pickle gravy into the well. Steam for 8 to 10 minutes or until a toothpick comes out clean. (Idlies may also be microwaved; follow the instructions on page 42.) ✴ Gently loosen the edges with a knife, turn the cakes out, and arrange upright on a serving platter. Repeat with the remaining batter. ✴ VARIATIONS: I love hot mango pickle in this recipe. Experiment with your favorite Indian pickle. My cousin, who taught me this recipe, adds grated ginger pickle. ✴ MAKES: 6

EACH SERVING PROVIDES (3 IDLIES PER SERVING): CALORIES: 143; PROTEIN: 5 G; CARBOHYDRATES: 29 G; FAT: 2 G

Idlies are a staple in South Indian homes and have over the years gained a lot of popularity in the rest of the country and the rest of the world. They can be eaten at mealtimes or with afternoon tea.

You can buy a packaged dry mix or cooked frozen idlies at Indian grocery stores (of course, the frozen ones are plain and do not have the stuffing).

Tips: Ensure that there are no large pieces of pickle in the gravy, otherwise the semolina puffs will not steam well.

Always add ENO just before you cook the cakes.

My aunt Meena, who lives in Toronto, taught me how to make these crepes. The batter keeps for up to a week.

Tips: Since this batter keeps well in the fridge for up to a week and also freezes well, this recipe makes twice the amount you need for one meal.

Use a large bowl when fermenting the rice and the dal because the batter is likely to increase in size when fermenting.

If the crêpes stick in the skillet, rub the skillet with a halved potato or onion dipped in oil.

indian crêpes with potato filling (dosa)

Prep Time: Overnight, plus 5 to 6 hours for fermenting
Cooking Time: 35 minutes

FOR THE CRÊPE BATTER:
1 ½ cups / 375 mL basmati rice
½ cup / 125 mL urad dal

1 ½ teaspoons / 7 mL fenugreek seeds
Salt to taste

FOR THE FILLING:
1 tablespoon / 15 mL vegetable oil
1 teaspoon / 5 mL mustard seeds
3 or 4 curry leaves
1 small onion, chopped
1 green chile, chopped
1 cup / 250 mL boiled, peeled and coarsely mashed potatoes

1 tablespoon / 15 mL finely chopped fresh coriander
1 teaspoon / 5 mL grated ginger
½ teaspoon / 2 mL turmeric
Salt to taste

5 teaspoons / 25 mL vegetable oil

To make the crêpe batter, in a large bowl combine the rice, dal, and fenugreek seeds. Cover with water and soak overnight at room temperature. ❊ Drain the mixture and place in a blender with a few drops of water; blend to make a fine paste. Add the salt. Return to the bowl. Set aside in a warm place for at least 6 hours or until the mixture ferments. The batter should have numerous tiny bubbles after it ferments. Do not stir this batter more than once or twice. ❊ To make the filling, in a medium skillet over medium heat, heat 1 tablespoon / 15 mL oil. Add the mustard seeds. As soon as they begin to crackle, add the curry leaves and the onion. Sauté for 2 to 3 minutes or until the onions are transparent. Add the green chile, mashed potatoes, coriander, ginger, turmeric, and salt. Mix well. Cook, stirring occasionally, for 3 minutes. Remove from the heat. ❊ To make the crêpes, heat a large nonstick skillet over medium heat. Sprinkle on a few drops of water; if they sizzle, the pan is ready. Add a teaspoon of oil and smear the skillet (use very little oil or the batter will stick). Lower the heat to medium-low. ❊ Pour about 3 tablespoons / 45 mL of batter into the skillet. Spread the batter very thinly by moving the ladle in concentric circles through the batter. As the batter cooks, bubbles will begin to appear on the surface. Pour a teaspoon of oil along the sides. When the underside is golden, use a spatula to loosen the crêpe from the skillet. Do not flip the crêpe. Spread about 1 tablespoon / 15 mL of the filling on one side of the crêpe. Fold the other half over. Slide the crêpe onto a plate. Repeat with remaining batter to make 4 crêpes. ❊ Serve hot with Coconut Chutney (page 96) and Red Lentil Curry (page 95). ❊ VARIATIONS: Two family favorites are paneer filling and ground meat filling (even though these crêpes are traditionally vegetarian fare). For the paneer filling, replace the potato with 1 cup / 250 mL of grated paneer. For the ground meat filling, replace the potato with about ½ pound / 250 g of ground meat and cook for about 10 minutes. Omit the curry leaves and mustard seeds; add 1 chopped small tomato when the onions become transparent. ❋ Makes: 4 crêpes (with half the batter)

Each Serving Provides (2 crêpes per serving): Calories: 330; Protein: 8 g; Carbohydrates: 60 g; Fat: 7 g

red lentil curry (sambar)*

Prep Time: 10 minutes
Cooking Time: 30 minutes

- -

7 cups / 1.75 L water
½ cup / 125 mL toor dal
1 ¼ teaspoons / 6 mL turmeric
Salt to taste
1 tablespoon / 15 mL vegetable oil
Pinch of asafetida
5 or 6 curry leaves
2 teaspoons / 10 mL ground coriander
1 teaspoon / 5 mL mustard seeds
½ teaspoon / 2 mL fenugreek seeds

½ teaspoon / 2 mL sambar powder
1 large tomato, chopped
1 cup / 250 mL mixed vegetables (such as diced eggplant, chopped onion, diced potato)
1 tablespoon / 15 mL tamarind paste, dissolved in some warm water
1 tablespoon / 15 mL unsweetened desiccated coconut
1 teaspoon / 5 mL salt

In a medium saucepan bring 2 cups / 500 mL of the water, the dal, 1 teaspoon / 5 mL of the turmeric, and salt to a boil. Cook until the dal is soft and mushy (about 10 minutes). Remove from the heat. Add 2 cups / 500 mL water. Using a hand blender, blend the mixture until almost completely smooth. ❋ In a medium saucepan over medium heat, heat the oil. Add the asafetida, curry leaves, coriander, mustard seeds, fenugreek seeds, and sambar powder. When the mustard seeds begin to crackle, add the tomato and vegetables. Sauté for 1 minute. Add the tamarind paste, remaining ¼ teaspoon / 1 mL turmeric, the coconut, salt, and remaining 3 cups / 750 mL water. Bring to a boil. Lower the heat and simmer, covered and stirring occasionally, until the vegetables are fully cooked (about 10 minutes). ❋ Add the cooked dal and simmer for another few minutes until heated through. Serve hot with Indian Crêpes. ❋ Variations: Instead of the vegetables, use peeled pearl onions for a curry with a distinctive flavor. This dish is native to South India, where another commonly used vegetable is okra. ❋ Yield: 2 servings (with leftovers)

Each Serving Provides: Calories: 186; Protein: 9 g; Carbohydrates: 24 g; Fat: 7 g

The MTR brand of sambar powder is divine. Buy it from your local Indian grocer or order it from ethnicsuperstore.com.

Tips: Sambar freezes well, but if you are making enough to freeze, do not add potatoes. They lose their structure when frozen and will not taste good in the curry.

Coconut grows well in the tropical climate of South India, so coconut milk and grated coconut are common in the region's cuisine. Use it sparingly, since it is high in fat.

Tips: For a true Indian taste, use fresh coconut. If you cannot find fresh coconut, you may substitute unsweetened desiccated coconut.

coconut chutney

Prep Time: 10 minutes
Cooking Time: 10 minutes

3 green chiles, chopped
1-inch / 2.5-cm piece peeled ginger, chopped
½ cup / 125 mL freshly grated coconut

½ cup / 125 mL chopped fresh coriander
3 tablespoons / 45 mL Bengal gram dal
Salt to taste

FOR THE TADKA:
2 teaspoons / 10 mL oil
1 teaspoon / 5 mL mustard seeds
½ teaspoon / 2 mL cumin seeds

3 or 4 curry leaves
1 to 2 dried red chiles, broken
Pinch of asafetida

IN a blender, blend the green chiles, ginger, coconut, coriander, dal, and salt until coarse. Set aside. ✳ To make the tadka, heat the oil in a small nonstick skillet over medium heat. Add the mustard seeds, cumin seeds, curry leaves, red chiles, and asafetida. When the mustard seeds begin to crackle, remove from the heat and stir into the coconut paste. ✳ Serve with Indian Crêpes or Steamed Semolina Puffs. ✳ VARIATIONS: To the blender, add 1 cup / 250 mL of chopped mint leaves to give the chutney a fresh flavor. Or for a more exotic taste, add 1 tablespoon / 15 mL of tamarind paste. ✳ MAKES: 1 cup / 250 mL. Serving size is 2 teaspoons / 10 mL.
EACH SERVING PROVIDES: CALORIES: 37; PROTEIN: TRACE; CARBOHYDRATES: 2 G; FAT: 3 G

According to an old Hindu legend, the forbidden fruit was the banana, not the apple! It has also been called the "Fruit of the Wise Man."

Tips: This dish will keep in an airtight container for about 3 or 4 days in the fridge.

sweet bananas

Prep Time: 5 minutes
Cooking Time: 20 minutes

2 small bananas, peeled
¼ cup / 60 mL sugar
1 tablespoon / 15 mL vegetable oil

Pinch of cinnamon
A drop of yellow food coloring

IN a bowl, mash the bananas. Add the sugar, oil, cinnamon, and yellow food coloring. Stir well. ✳ Lightly grease a serving platter. ✳ Heat a nonstick skillet over low heat. Add the banana mixture and cook, stirring constantly, until the mixture starts to thicken and leaves the sides of the pan. Remove from the heat. Turn onto a cutting board and let cool. ✳ Using a knife, cut into 8 shapes of your choice. Transfer to a platter and serve. ✳ VARIATIONS: Add ½ tablespoon / 7 mL of ground walnuts for a crunchier texture. ✳ YIELD: 8 bite-sized pieces
EACH SERVING PROVIDES: CALORIES: 78; PROTEIN: TRACE; CARBOHYDRATES: 15 G; FAT: 2 G

WEB BITES | Check out Banana Bobby on Dole's Web site for some interesting banana facts: http://www.dole.com/bobby/bananas/index.html

egg-coated semolina puffs

. . . .

IF you have any of these puffs left over, try this recipe from a dear cousin. She coats the cooked puffs with a beaten egg and then panfries them for a wonderful snack with afternoon tea.

coconut chutney sandwiches

. . . .

FOR each sandwich, lightly butter 1 slice of bread. Spread about 2 teaspoons / 10 mL of the chutney on a second slice. Sprinkle some peanut spice rub (page 78) on the buttered bread, if you like. Cover with the chutney-covered slice. Cut the sandwich in half diagonally and serve.

Serves 6

I LOVE THANKSGIVING. I love the advertisements on TV about families being together. But I didn't always. When I first moved to the States, I was a poor lonely graduate student with no family here. It was hard for me to watch everyone going home to be with their family for the holiday. There is a lesson here: if you know any poor lonely foreign graduate students, invite them over for a holiday meal. Trust me, they will thank you for it. ❈ Although I love the tradition itself, I am not a big turkey fan. It's too mild for my taste. So I rewrote the traditional recipe and basted it in Indian spices. I now present it to you my way to try for yourself.

◈ =EXPRESS MENU

turkey day

I know I will get a lot of letters about how surprisingly good this tea tastes.

Tips: This tea is traditionally served in small 4-ounce / 125-mL cups. The spices are strong, so the portions are small!

no tea leaves tea (kashmiri chai)

Prep Time: 5 minutes
Cooking Time: 5 minutes

4 cardamom pods, bruised
1 small cinnamon stick
Few saffron threads

4 cups / 1 L boiling water
2 tablespoons / 25 mL slivered almonds
Honey to taste

PUT the cardamom pods, cinnamon, and saffron in a teapot. Pour the boiling water over the spices. Let steep for about 5 minutes. ❄ Place a teaspoonful of almonds in each of 6 small teacups. Pour the tea over the almonds, sweeten to taste with honey, and serve immediately. ❄ VARIATIONS: This is a variation of traditional Kashmiri tea. To make the original, steep the spice mixture with about 2 teaspoons / 10 mL of green Kashmiri tea.
EACH SERVING PROVIDES: CALORIES: 65; PROTEIN: 1 G; CARBOHYDRATES: 8 G; FAT: 3 G

The use of paneer makes these starters taste almost silken.

Tips: You can also grill these kebabs.

The uncooked marinated kebabs freeze well. When ready to use, simply defrost and roast.

chicken cheese kebabs
(murgi paneer kebabs)*

Prep Time: 15 minutes, plus 4 hours for marinating
Cooking Time: 25 minutes

¼ cup / 60 mL finely grated paneer
¼ cup / 60 mL low-fat plain yogurt
2 tablespoons / 25 mL ginger garlic paste
1 ½ tablespoons / 20 mL finely
    chopped fresh coriander
1 teaspoon / 5 mL red chile powder
2 green chiles, seeded and finely chopped

1 egg, beaten
Salt to taste
1 pound / 500 g skinless, boneless chicken
    breasts, cubed
2 teaspoons / 10 mL vegetable oil
Garnish: Thinly sliced onions and
    lemon wedges

IN a medium bowl, stir together the paneer, yogurt, ginger garlic paste, coriander, chile powder, green chiles, egg, and salt. Add the chicken and turn to coat well. Marinate, covered and refrigerated, for 3 to 4 hours. ❄ Preheat the oven to 400°F / 200°C. Lightly grease a baking sheet. ❄ Thread the chicken onto 3 skewers and place on the baking sheet. Roast for 8 to 12 minutes or until the chicken is cooked through. Baste with the oil; roast for 1 minute more. ❄ Garnish with onions and lemon wedges and serve with your choice of chutney. ❄ VARIATIONS: If you're watching your cholesterol, you can omit the egg and add a teaspoon of lemon juice to the marinade.
EACH SERVING PROVIDES: CALORIES: 153; PROTEIN: 21 G; CARBOHYDRATES: 3 G; FAT: 6 G

minted lamb patties (ghost kebab)*

Prep Time: 35 minutes
Cooking Time: 25 minutes

. . . .

1 pound / 500 g ground lamb
3 tablespoons / 45 mL dry roasted gram
flour (see Tips)
2 tablespoons / 25 mL fat-free plain yogurt
1 tablespoon / 15 mL finely chopped
fresh mint

1 tablespoon / 15 mL ginger garlic paste
1 tablespoon / 15 mL oil
2 teaspoons / 10 mL black peppercorns
2 teaspoons / 10 mL heavy cream
½ teaspoon / 2 mL red chile powder
Salt to taste

IN a mixing bowl, combine the lamb, gram flour, yogurt, mint, ginger garlic paste, oil, peppercorns, cream, chile powder, and salt. Knead to mix well. Let stand for about 15 minutes. ❉ Preheat the oven to 375°F / 190°C. Lightly grease a baking sheet. ❉ Moisten your hands and make 6 equal small flat patties. Place the patties on the baking sheet. ❉ Bake for 10 to 12 minutes or until browned and cooked through, turning the patties halfway through the cooking time to ensure even browning. ❉ VARIATIONS: For a totally different flavor, replace the mint with 1 tablespoon / 15 mL of dried fenugreek leaves. Traditionally these kebabs are panfried.
EACH SERVING PROVIDES: CALORIES: 167; PROTEIN: 18 G; CARBOHYDRATES: 7 G; FAT: 7 G

tandoori turkey*

Prep Time: 25 minutes, plus marinating overnight
Cooking Time: 3 hours

. . . .

1 (8- to 10-pound) turkey

¼ cup / 60 mL chicken stock

FOR THE MARINADE:
1 cup / 250 mL low-fat plain yogurt
2 tablespoons / 25 mL ginger garlic paste
1 teaspoon / 5 mL crushed red chiles

1 green chile, chopped
Salt to taste

FOR THE FILLING:
1 tablespoon / 15 mL vegetable oil
1 onion, finely chopped
2-inch / 5-cm piece peeled ginger, grated
2 green chiles, seeded and finely chopped
2 tablespoons / 25 mL finely chopped
fresh coriander
2 tablespoons / 25 mL finely chopped
fresh mint

1 cup / 250 mL finely ground mutton
1 teaspoon / 5 mL garam masala
1 teaspoon / 5 mL cumin seeds
1 teaspoon / 5 mL turmeric
Salt to taste
1 cup / 250 mL cooked basmati rice
1 tablespoon / 15 mL slivered blanched
almonds

CONTINUED . . .

You can also make these patties with ground beef, turkey, or chicken.

Tips: To dry roast gram flour: Heat a nonstick skillet over medium-low heat. Add the gram flour. Sauté for a few minutes until fragrant. Remove from the heat and let cool.

Turkey is not traditionally served in India, and this recipe is a result of 10 years of experimentation. Some friends of mine have a Thanksgiving tradition that had a lasting impression on me. After dinner, there was a sundae bar, where you made your most favorite sundae. Then you turned around and gave it to someone you loved.

FOR THE GRAVY:

1 tablespoon / 15 mL vegetable oil	2 tablespoons / 25 mL fried onion paste
1 tablespoon / 15 mL ginger garlic paste	Salt to taste
1 cup / 250 mL fat-free plain yogurt, whipped	

PRICK the turkey all over with a fork. Place the turkey on a rack in a roasting pan. ✳ To make the marinade, in a small bowl combine the yogurt, ginger garlic paste, crushed chiles, green chile, and salt. Rub marinade evenly into the turkey. Cover and refrigerate for at least 12 hours or overnight. ✳ Preheat the oven to 400°F / 200°C. ✳ To prepare the filling: Heat the oil in a nonstick skillet over medium-high heat. Add the onion, ginger, and green chiles; sauté until the onions are golden brown. Add the coriander and mint; sauté for 1 minute. Add the mutton, garam masala, cumin seeds, turmeric, and salt to taste. Cook, stirring frequently, until well browned. Stir in the rice and almonds. Remove from the heat. ✳ Stuff the turkey with the filling. Add the chicken stock to the pan. Roast the turkey, uncovered, for 15 minutes per pound, basting occasionally with the chicken stock. Halfway through the cooking time, reduce the heat to 325°F / 160°C. The turkey will be golden brown all over when done. ✳ Remove the turkey from the oven and tent with foil to keep warm. Drain the pan juices into a measuring cup. Skim off the fat from the juices. ✳ To prepare the gravy: Heat the oil in a medium saucepan over medium heat. Add the ginger garlic paste and cook briefly, stirring, until fragrant. Remove the pan from heat. Stir in the yogurt and fried onion paste; stir-fry until the oil leaves the sides of the pan. ✳ Add the reserved pan juices and salt; bring to a boil, stirring occasionally. Lower the heat and simmer, stirring occasionally, until the gravy reaches sauce consistency. Pour the gravy through a fine sieve into a bowl. ✳ Serve the gravy on the side with the turkey. ✳ VARIATIONS: Instead of the yogurt and onion paste, you can add 1 cup / 250 mL of chopped peeled tomatoes. ✳ YIELD: 6 servings, with lots of leftovers

EACH SERVING PROVIDES (INCLUDES 2 TABLESPOONS / 25 ML GRAVY): CALORIES: 560; PROTEIN: 86 G; CARBOHYDRATES: 12 G; FAT: 14 G

WEB BITES | This informative article on roasting turkeys provides a helpful chart of cooking times: http://www.homestore.com/food_recipes/cooking/holiday/thanksgiving/roasting.asp

Check out http://www.learn2.com for simple techniques on roasting a bird.

spicy chicken bake
(tandoori chicken)*

Prep Time: 25 minutes, plus 2 hours for marinating
Cooking Time: 35 minutes

. . . .

½ cup / 125 mL low-fat plain yogurt
½ cup / 125 mL hung plain yogurt
  (page 20)
1 tablespoon / 15 mL crushed garlic
1 tablespoon / 15 mL grated ginger
1 tablespoon / 15 mL vegetable oil
1 tablespoon / 15 mL lemon juice
1 teaspoon / 5 mL garam masala

1 teaspoon / 5 mL red chile powder
Few drops of red food coloring
Salt to taste
6 skinless chicken thighs or drumsticks
2 teaspoons / 10 mL melted butter
Garnish: Pinch of chaat masala, sliced
  onions, and lemon wedges

IN a mixing bowl, combine the yogurt, hung yogurt, garlic, ginger, oil, lemon juice, garam masala, chile powder, red food coloring, and salt. Cut deep slits in the chicken pieces to allow the marinade to penetrate. Put the chicken in a roasting pan and rub the marinade all over it. Marinate, covered and refrigerated, for at least 2 hours. ❋ Preheat the oven to 400°F / 200°C. ❋ Roast the chicken for 10 to 12 minutes or until cooked through, basting occasionally with the butter. ❋ Serve hot, sprinkled with chaat masala and garnished with onion slices and lemon wedges. ❋ VARIATIONS: Make a small pouch in the marinated thigh by cutting into the flesh to create a small flap. Add 1 teaspoon / 5 mL of grated paneer to the pouch, cover with the flesh, and bake for a delicious meal in itself! EACH SERVING PROVIDES: CALORIES: 141; PROTEIN: 19 G; CARBOHYDRATES: 3 G; FAT: 6 G

Any Indian restaurant worth its name will have this famous chicken dish on its menu. It has become standard fare because of its wonderful succulent taste. Incidentally, yogurt is used not only to flavor the dish but also as a tenderizer.

Tips: Many Indian stores sell tandoori masalas or pastes. I prefer the dried masalas to the pastes, but try both and see which pleases your palate.

This is my version of the green bean casserole that is part of a traditional Thanksgiving meal.

Tips: Do not over-cook the beans or they will lose color and texture. If you are using frozen beans, you can save cooking time by precooking the beans in the micro-wave. Skip the stage of adding the water and cooking.

indian green beans with grated coconut*

Prep Time: 5 minutes
Cooking Time: 25 minutes

1 tablespoon / 15 mL vegetable oil
1 teaspoon / 5 mL mustard seeds
Pinch of asafetida
½ pound / 250 g chopped green beans (fresh or frozen)
1 dried red chile
½ teaspoon / 2 mL turmeric
½ teaspoon / 2 mL red chile powder
1 cup / 250 mL water
Salt to taste
2 tablespoons / 25 mL finely chopped fresh coriander
1 tablespoon / 15 mL unsweetened desiccated coconut
1 teaspoon / 5 mL butter

IN a large nonstick skillet, heat the oil over medium heat. Add the mustard seeds and asafetida. When the mustard seeds begin to crackle, add the green beans. Sauté for 1 minute. Add the dried chile, turmeric, and chile powder. Sauté for 2 minutes. ❋ Add the water and salt. Cook, uncovered, until the beans are tender and all the water is absorbed (about 10 minutes). Add the coriander, coconut, and butter; sauté for about another minute to mix all the flavors. ❋ Serve hot. ❋ VARIATIONS: You can add ½ cup / 125 mL of diced potatoes to this dish. Add the potatoes before adding the green beans and sauté for 3 to 4 minutes. Then add the green beans and continue with the recipe.
EACH SERVING PROVIDES: CALORIES: 56; PROTEIN: 1 G; CARBOHYDRATES: 2 G; FAT: 5 G

Chutneys can be made with many fruits. Try mango, pineapple, raspberry, or even apples. This chutney freezes well.

Tips: As soon as the chutney starts to thicken remove it from the heat. It will continue to thicken after it has cooked. If the cranberries are too sour, add a bit more sugar to taste.

cranberry chutney

Prep Time: 5 minutes
Cooking Time: 20 minutes

½ pound / 250 g fresh or frozen cranberries
1 cup / 250 mL water
¾ cup / 175 mL sugar
2 teaspoons / 10 mL cinnamon
1 teaspoon / 5 mL chopped walnuts
1 teaspoon / 5 mL ground ginger
¼ teaspoon / 1 mL ground cloves
¼ teaspoon / 1 mL garam masala

IN a medium saucepan, combine the cranberries, water, sugar, cinnamon, walnuts, ginger, cloves, and garam masala. Bring to boil, stirring constantly. Reduce heat and simmer for 10 to 15 minutes until mixture thickens. Remove from the heat and mash the berries with a potato masher. Let cool completely and store in the refrigerator for up to 2 weeks. ❋ VARIATIONS: You can add coarsely chopped dry roasted peanuts instead of the walnuts. ❋ YIELD: 2 cups / 500 mL. Serving size is 2 tablespoons / 25 mL.
EACH SERVING PROVIDES: CALORIES: 57; PROTEIN: TRACE; CARBOHYDRATES: 11 G; FAT: 1 G

pumpkin basket salad

Prep Time: 5 minutes
Cooking Time: None

. . . .

1 cup / 250 mL fat-free plain yogurt
¼ cup / 60 mL mashed cooked
   pumpkin (fresh or canned)
1 tablespoon / 15 mL ground
   roasted peanuts

1 teaspoon / 5 mL sugar
Salt to taste
Garnish: Fresh coriander leaves

In a medium bowl combine the yogurt, pumpkin, peanuts, sugar, and salt. Mix well. Garnish with a few coriander leaves. The pumpkin salad is ready! ❋ VARIATIONS: You can replace the pumpkin with cooked grated carrots.

EACH SERVING PROVIDES: CALORIES: 50; PROTEIN: 3 G; CARBOHYDRATES: 8 G; FAT: 1 G

Serve this salad in a hollowed-out pumpkin. (That's the basket part!)

pumpkin halwa with crêpes

Prep Time: 20 minutes
Cooking Time: 20 minutes

. . . .

FOR THE FILLING:
1 cup / 250 mL cooked pumpkin
   (fresh or canned)
1 cup / 250 mL low-fat heavy cream

2 tablespoons / 25 mL confectioner's sugar
1 teaspoon / 5 mL cinnamon
½ teaspoon / 2 mL ground nutmeg

FOR THE CRÊPES:
1 cup / 250 mL all-purpose flour
½ cup / 125 mL sugar
½ cup / 125 mL 1% milk

¼ teaspoon / 1 mL baking soda
Pinch of fennel essence (optional)
3 tablespoons / 45 mL vegetable oil

TO prepare the filling: In a small saucepan, combine the pumpkin and cream; cook over medium heat, stirring constantly, until the mixture boils and becomes very thick. Let cool completely. Add the confectioner's sugar, cinnamon, and nutmeg; mix well. Set aside. ❋ To prepare the crêpes: In a mixing bowl combine the flour, sugar, milk, baking soda, and fennel essence; stir to obtain a thin batter. ❋ Heat a small nonstick skillet over medium heat. Pour in 2 tablespoons / 25 mL batter to make a thin, crêpe-like pancake about 4 or 5 inches / 10 or 12 cm across. Add ¼ teaspoon / 1 mL of oil along the edges to prevent the crêpe from sticking. When bubbles appear on the top and the edges are dry, flip the crêpe over. Cook for another minute. Transfer crêpe to a plate. Repeat with remaining batter to make 8 crêpes. ❋ To assemble, place 2 to 3 tablespoons / 25 to 45 mL pumpkin filling in the center of each crêpe. Fold in half. Serve at room temperature.

Serve these crêpes dusted lightly with confectioner's sugar for a professional touch.

CONTINUED . . .

✳ VARIATIONS: For a non-pumpkin version, use 1 cup / 250 mL of cooked grated carrots in place of the pumpkin.

EACH SERVING PROVIDES: CALORIES: 142; PROTEIN: 4 G; CARBOHYDRATES: 36 G; FAT: 2 G

WEB BITES | All you ever wanted to know about pumpkins but were afraid to ask: http://www.urbanext.uiuc.edu/pumpkins/index.html

chicken with butter and cream sauce

THIS is my all-time favorite dish. Bone any remaining tandoori chicken. In a nonstick skillet heat 2 tablespoons / 25 mL of butter over medium heat. Add 1 ½ cups / 375 mL chopped tomatoes and 1 tablespoon / 15 mL coarsely grated ginger. Cook until the tomatoes are soft (about 5 minutes). Add chile powder and salt to taste. Add the chicken; sauté for about a minute. Add 2 tablespoons / 25 mL of low-fat heavy cream. Stir well. Sauté for another minute. Remove from the heat. Top with finely chopped fresh coriander and 2 teaspoons / 10 mL of heavy cream, and serve with a hot naan or freshly steamed white rice.

Both my parents are awesome cooks. My dad is a whiz on the grill. When I was a lot older and wiser, I realized why his dishes were never the same twice in a row. One day I watched him as he made the marinade for a chicken dish. He kept (confidently) picking jars from the spice rack and adding whatever he could reach. After he left the kitchen, I took an inventory of what he had added: tandoori masala, pizza seasoning, black salt, and cumin seeds. It was the first time we ever had pizza seasoning in the house. The chicken tasted great, and his secret stayed safe with me. Until now. ✳ This menu is a tribute to my parents. It includes their most delicious recipes. Try them out, and add ingredients of your own to make them your own special recipes.

Serves 4

backyard grilling

bottoms up

getting started

where's the real food?

on the side

live a little

heavenly leftovers

◈ = EXPRESS MENU

The Indian name for this drink means lemon water. Many folks in India keep a small bottle of lemon juice and sugar mix in the fridge and add cold water when they want a truly refreshing drink.

Tips: To make juicing a lemon easier, first roll it on a board. Then heat it in the microwave for about 3 seconds.

If you use wooden skewers, soak them in water for at least 45 minutes before you use them.

Tips: Make sure you oil the grill before heating to ensure that the food does not stick.

indian lemonade (nimbu pani)

Prep Time: 5 minutes
Cooking Time: None

3 large lemons
1 tablespoon / 15 mL sugar
4 cups / 1 L cold water

2½ teaspoons / 12 mL rose water
Garnish: Crushed ice and red rose petals

SQUEEZE the juice from the lemons into a mixing bowl. Add the sugar and mix well to dissolve the sugar. Add the water and rose water; mix well. Pour into chilled glasses. Serve with crushed ice and a few rose petals in each glass. ✳ VARIATIONS: Instead of the rose water and rose petals, make a different summer cooler by adding ¼ teaspoon / 1 mL crushed cumin seeds and a pinch each of salt and black pepper. Garnish with mint leaves.
EACH SERVING PROVIDES: CALORIES: 27; PROTEIN: TRACE; CARBOHYDRATES: 6 G; FAT: TRACE

WEB BITES | This article provides some tasty recipes using lemon juice:
http://www.consciouschoice.com/cooking/cooking1205.html

lamb kebabs

Prep: 10 minutes, plus 2 hours for marinating
Cooking Time: 20 minutes

1 cup / 250 mL hung fat-free
   plain yogurt (page 20)
2 tablespoons / 25 mL finely
   chopped fresh coriander
1 tablespoon / 15 mL lemon juice
1 tablespoon / 15 mL ginger garlic paste

1 teaspoon / 5 mL chaat masala
1 teaspoon / 5 mL garam masala
1 green chile, finely chopped
1 pound / 500 g cubed lamb
2 teaspoons / 10 mL vegetable oil

IN a bowl stir together well the yogurt, coriander, lemon juice, ginger garlic paste, chaat masala, garam masala, and green chile. Add the lamb, turning to coat. Marinate, covered and refrigerated, for about 2 hours. ✳ Preheat the grill. ✳ Thread the lamb onto skewers. Grill for 10 to 12 minutes or until lamb is tender, basting with the oil and turning occasionally to ensure even cooking. ✳ Remove lamb from skewers and serve hot with mint chutney (page 76). ✳ VARIATIONS: This marinade is good with any white fish and with beef.
EACH SERVING PROVIDES: CALORIES: 216; PROTEIN: 26 G; CARBOHYDRATES: 7 G; FAT: 9 G

WEB BITES | Here is the *Better Homes and Gardens* guide to grilling:
http://www.bhg.com/food/grillguide/grilltips.htm

mustard fish**

Prep Time: 15 minutes, plus 1 hour for marinating
Cooking Time: 10 minutes

4 fillets (about 1 pound / 500 g)
   whitefish (such as catfish or tilapia)
3 tablespoons / 45 mL lemon juice
½ cup / 125 mL chopped fresh coriander
1 tablespoon / 15 mL mustard seeds,
   coarsely crushed
1 tablespoon / 15 mL vegetable oil

½ teaspoon / 2 mL red chile powder
¼ teaspoon / 1 mL garam masala
¼ teaspoon / 1 mL turmeric
1-inch / 2.5-cm piece peeled ginger
3 to 4 cloves garlic
Salt to taste
Garnish: Sliced onion and lemon wedges

RUB the fish with 1 tablespoon / 15 mL of the lemon juice; set aside for 10 minutes. ✳ In a blender combine the remaining 2 tablespoons / 25 mL lemon juice, coriander, mustard seeds, oil, chile powder, garam masala, turmeric, ginger, garlic, and salt; blend to a smooth paste. Transfer the paste to a bowl. ✳ Rub this paste onto the fish. Cover and refrigerate for at least 1 hour. ✳ Preheat the grill. ✳ Cook the fillets on the grill until lightly browned on the bottom, about 3 to 4 minutes. ✳ Carefully turn the fillets and cook for another 3 to 4 minutes or until fish flakes easily with a fork. ✳ Serve hot with sliced onions and lemon wedges. ✳ VARIATIONS: You can make fish tikka by omitting the mustard seeds and adding about ½ cup / 125 mL light (5%) cream to the marinade.
EACH SERVING PROVIDES: CALORIES: 165; PROTEIN: 28 G; CARBOHYDRATES: 5 G; FAT: 8 G

The mustard seeds give this dish a nice nutty flavor.

Tips: Fish fillets are very delicate. Carefully turn them only once to avoid breaking them.

For a true Indian taste, use mustard oil instead of regular vegetable oil.

chicken tikka*

Prep Time: 15 minutes, plus 3 to 4 hours for marinating
Cooking Time: 20 minutes

1 cup / 250 mL fat-free plain yogurt
2 tablespoons / 25 mL lemon juice
1 tablespoon / 15 mL finely chopped
   fresh coriander
1 tablespoon / 15 mL ginger garlic paste
1 teaspoon / 5 mL ground coriander
1 teaspoon / 5 mL red chile powder

½ teaspoon / 2 mL ground cumin
½ teaspoon / 2 mL white pepper
1 pound / 500 g skinless, boneless chicken
   breasts, cut into 1-inch / 2.5-cm cubes
1 tablespoon / 15 mL vegetable oil
Garnish: Onion rings

IN a medium bowl combine the yogurt, lemon juice, fresh coriander, ginger garlic paste, ground coriander, chile powder, cumin, and pepper; mix well. Add the chicken, turning to coat. Marinate, covered and refrigerated, for about 3 hours. ✳ Preheat the grill. ✳ Thread the chicken onto skewers. Grill for 8 to 10 minutes or until chicken is cooked through, turning skewers occasionally and basting with cooking oil. ✳ Remove tikka from skewers. Serve garnished with onion rings. ✳ VARIATIONS: This is also a wonderful marinade for shrimp.
EACH SERVING PROVIDES: CALORIES: 173; PROTEIN: 14 G; CARBOHYDRATES: 3 G; FAT: 7 G

Use any leftovers in a pita along with shredded lettuce and sliced tomato for the Indian version of a grilled chicken sandwich.

Tips: My mother always uses the remaining marinade to baste the chicken instead of using oil. If you do it this way, make sure that the marinade gets cooked fully.

This recipe happened quite by accident when I once forgot to add chicken to the mix.

Tips: I like to use the ready-made foil bags for this dish.

The cooking time will vary depending on the size of the potatoes and the heat of the grill. Initially, I recommend trying the cooking time indicated. If the potatoes are not done, close the packet and grill again.

baby potato and garlic packets

Prep Time: 40 minutes
Cooking Time: 20 minutes

1 cup / 250 mL finely chopped
    fresh coriander
1 tablespoon / 15 mL vegetable oil
1 tablespoon / 15 mL ginger garlic paste
1 teaspoon / 5 mL ground cumin
1 teaspoon / 5 mL red chile powder

1 small onion, grated
2 green chiles, chopped
Salt to taste
1 ½ pounds / 750 g small red potatoes,
    rinsed and dried
8 cloves garlic

IN a bowl, combine the coriander, oil, ginger garlic paste, cumin, chile powder, onion, green chiles, and salt. Prick the potatoes all over with a fork. Stir the potatoes and garlic into the marinade and set aside for about 20 minutes. ✳ Preheat the grill. ✳ Cut out 4 sheets of foil. Place equal amounts of potato mixture in the center of each piece of foil. Cut another 4 sheets of foil. Place each on top of the potatoes. Firmly fold over the ends to form sealed packets. ✳ Put the package above the hottest part of the grill. Cook, covered, for 20 minutes. Flip the packets over and cook for another 10 minutes or until potatoes are tender. ✳ Open the packets carefully — the steam will be very hot. Serve warm. ✳ VARIATIONS: Add your choice of vegetables to the packets. You can also skewer the marinated vegetables instead of placing them in packets.
EACH SERVING PROVIDES: CALORIES: 100; PROTEIN: 2 G; CARBOHYDRATES: 15 G; FAT: 4 G

When I was growing up, we would always spend summers in India, and one thing I always looked forward to was eating corn on the cob from Delhi street vendors. They roast it on an open fire or boil it, then add mouthwatering spices along with lemon juice. This is my tribute to them. Many recipes call for grilling corn in its husk, but I prefer to grill husked corn.

corn on the cob with spicy rub**

Prep Time: 5 minutes
Cooking Time: 10 minutes

4 corn cobs, husked
½ lemon

1 tablespoon / 15 mL chaat masala

PLACE the corn (with the husks) in cold water for at least an hour, and remove the husks before grilling. Preheat the grill. Grill the corn, turning frequently with tongs, until black spots start appearing on the corn. ✳ Remove corn from the grill. Squeeze half a lemon over the cobs. Rub about a teaspoon / 5 mL (or less to taste) of the chaat masala all over the corn. ✳ Serve immediately. ✳ VARIATIONS: Try a garlic spice rub or Cajun seasoning instead of the chaat masala.
EACH SERVING PROVIDES: CALORIES: 67; PROTEIN: 2 G; CARBOHYDRATES: 16 G; FAT: TRACE

mint chutney II

Prep Time: 10 minutes
Cooking Time: 10 minutes

• •

1 cup / 250 mL packed fresh
  coriander leaves
½ cup / 125 mL packed fresh mint leaves
1 tablespoon / 15 mL lemon juice

1 green chile
2 cloves garlic
Salt to taste

IN a blender, combine the coriander, mint, lemon juice, green chile, garlic, and salt; blend until smooth. Add a tablespoon / 15 mL of water for a thinner consistency, if desired. Transfer to a storage container. ❋ VARIATIONS: Add 1 chopped small mango to give the chutney a different texture and taste. ❋ YIELD: About 2 cups / 500 mL. Serving size is 2 tablespoons / 25 mL.
EACH SERVING PROVIDES: CALORIES: 12; PROTEIN: 1 G; CARBOHYDRATES: 2 G; FAT: TRACE

pickled onions

Prep Time: 10 minutes, plus 48 hours to set
Cooking Time: None

• •

1 cup / 250 mL pearl onions, boiled
  and peeled
½ cup / 125 mL water
1 teaspoon / 5 mL mustard seeds, ground

½ teaspoon / 2 mL turmeric
1 green chile, seeded and chopped
Salt to taste

STIR together the onions, water, mustard seeds, turmeric, green chile, and salt. Place in an airtight container for 48 hours. Your pickle is ready. ❋ VARIATIONS: Use 1 cup / 250 mL of vinegar instead of the water, and add salt to taste and a pinch of red food coloring. Store in an airtight jar for about 48 hours. Your pink pickle is ready. ❋ YIELD: 1 cup / 250 mL. Serving size is 4 to 5 small onions.
EACH SERVING PROVIDES: CALORIES: 14; PROTEIN: TRACE; CARBOHYDRATES: 3; FAT: TRACE

Mint Chutney goes well with lamb. Try it with lamb chops.

Tips: This chutney can be used as a dipping sauce with many Indian appetizers.

This chutney freezes well for up to 4 months or keeps refrigerated, in an airtight container, for about a week.

This is one of my father's favorite pickles, and of course this is his version of the recipe.

Tips: These pickles have a short shelf life, only about a week.

n the hot summers of India, watermelon brings a welcome cool relief.

watermelon drizzled with honey

Prep Time: 10 minutes
Cooking Time: None

½ watermelon
1 tablespoon / 15 mL honey

Garnish: Chopped fresh mint

Cut the watermelon into thin slices. Place on a serving platter. Chill. Drizzle with honey. Serve garnished with mint. ❊ Variations: Add your favorite fruits to this dish. You can create a "boat" using the rind of the watermelon and serve the fruits in the boat.
Each Serving Provides: Calories: 20; Protein: Trace; Carbohydrates: 5 g; Fat: Trace

WEB BITES | Yes, all you watermelon lovers, there is an official Web site to promote watermelon: http://www.watermelon.org

kiwi sorbet

Prep Time: 5 minutes, plus chilling overnight
Cooking Time: 5 minutes

love the pale green color of this sorbet.

Tips: To make peeling a kiwi easier, slice both the ends off first. I have seen people use a paring knife to remove the peel. I have also seen a chef use a spoon. How? you ask. Simply visit the Web bite site I included at right!

½ cup / 125 mL water
2 tablespoons / 25 mL sugar

5 kiwi fruit, peeled and mashed

Combine water and sugar in a small saucepan and bring to a boil over medium heat, stirring constantly until the sugar has dissolved. Let cool. ❊ Purée the kiwis in a food processor. Combine the purée and the sugar syrup. Pour into an ice-cream maker and freeze according to manufacturer's instructions. ❊ Variations: Try this with litchi instead of kiwi. I have made ice cream with kiwi. Purée the kiwi and stir in a 14-ounce / 398-mL can of low-fat sweetened condensed milk. Freeze overnight in a square container, covered. Serve with slices of your favorite fresh fruit.
Each Serving Provides: Calories: 88; Protein: 1 g; Carbohydrates: 22 g; Fat: Trace

WEB BITES | Here's how to peel a kiwi with a spoon: http://www.cuisinemagazine.com/tips/cuitip11.html

potato soup

In a blender or food processor, combine leftover grilled potatoes and garlic, ½ a grated onion, ½ can (10 ounce / 284 mL) of chicken broth, 1 tablespoon / 15 mL all-purpose flour, and a pinch of black pepper. Cover and blend until nearly smooth. ❊ Pour the mixture into a medium saucepan. Stir in 1 cup / 250 mL of light (5%) cream. Cook, stirring, over medium heat until slightly thickened and bubbly. Ladle into soup bowls and serve immediately.

Serves 4
—※—

During my college years, I lived in a dorm in a Catholic convent with semi-cloistered nuns. I learnt a lot from them about the Catholic religion and also about the art of cooking in the south of India. They did not eat any meat on Fridays, so we were served the most delicious crab curries. ※ In this menu, I have combined some of the recipes from the convent with my own to give you a special meatless meal.

· · · · · · · · · · · ·

◈ = EXPRESS MENU

※

no-meat fridays

Indians are hot tea drinkers, a surprising fact given the warm climate of most of India. I first started drinking ice tea in America, strangely enough in the dead of winter.

Tips: Indian tea is best prepared with black tea leaves. Green tea or the Earl Grey teas are too mild and do not have the desired flavor.

indian spice ice tea (spice chai)

Prep Time: 2 minutes
Cooking Time: 6 minutes

1 cup / 250 mL water
2 tablespoons / 25 mL fennel seeds
Sugar to taste

2 cups / 500 mL prepared black tea
  (such as Indian Taj Mahal brand)

In a small saucepan, bring the water and fennel to a boil. Simmer for 2 to 3 minutes. Strain the liquid, discarding the fennel. In a jug, combine the fennel liquid, black tea, and sugar, stirring to dissolve the sugar. Serve chilled over crushed ice. ❅ VARIATIONS: I prefer to use honey instead of sugar with this ice tea.

EACH SERVING PROVIDES: CALORIES: 20; PROTEIN: TRACE; CARBOHYDRATES: 5 G; FAT: TRACE

In hindsight, I think this was my mother's way of making me eat all my vegetables when I was young. I never knew from one time to the next what she would put inside these wonderful patties.

Tips: Store semolina in the fridge, where it will stay fresh longer.

vegetable wonders*

Prep Time: 30 minutes
Cooking Time: 15 minutes

FOR THE DOUGH:
½ cup / 125 mL all-purpose flour
¼ cup / 60 mL chickpea flour
¼ cup / 60 mL semolina (sooji)

Salt to taste
1 tablespoon / 15 mL vegetable oil
1 cup / 250 mL warm water

FOR THE FILLING:
1 tablespoon / 15 mL vegetable oil
1 cup / 250 mL cooked mixed vegetables,
  finely chopped
1 green chile, finely chopped
1-inch / 2.5-cm piece peeled ginger, grated

1 teaspoon / 5 mL garam masala
½ teaspoon / 2 mL red chile powder
½ teaspoon / 2 mL ground coriander
¼ teaspoon / 1 mL mango powder

To make the dough, in a bowl combine the all-purpose flour, the chickpea flour, and the semolina. Stir in the salt and oil. Gradually add the water. Knead the mixture well to form a smooth dough. Set aside for 10 minutes. ❅ To make the filling, heat the oil in a large nonstick skillet over medium-high heat. Add the vegetables; sauté for 1 minute. Add the green chile, ginger, garam masala, chile powder, coriander, and mango powder; sauté for another 3 minutes. Remove from the heat. ❅ Preheat the oven to 200°F / 95°C. ❅ Divide the dough into 12 pieces and shape into balls. Using your finger, create a cavity in each ball. Add a heaping teaspoon of the vegetable mixture. Pinch the dough around the filling to enclose it. Gently flatten each ball between your palms to make a pattie. Be careful not to let the mixture break out of the dough. ✳ Place the filled patties on a baking sheet. Spray with vegetable cooking spray. Bake until the patties are browned on both sides (about 2 minutes per side), turning once. ✳ Serve warm with tomato ketchup. ✳ VARIATIONS: Instead of the vegetables, use cooked ground meat or cooked mixed lentils.

EACH SERVING PROVIDES (3 PIECES PER SERVING): CALORIES: 235; PROTEIN: 8 G; CARBOHYDRATES: 36 G; FAT: 8 G

crab curry**

Prep Time: 15 minutes
Cooking Time: 10 minutes

6 dried red chiles
1 teaspoon / 5 mL cumin seeds
1 teaspoon / 5 mL mustard seeds
¼ teaspoon / 1 mL turmeric
4 cloves garlic
1-inch / 2.5-cm piece peeled ginger
1 tablespoon / 15 mL vegetable oil
1 large onion, sliced
1 tablespoon / 15 mL unsweetened
   desiccated coconut

1 tablespoon / 15 mL tamarind paste, soaked
   in 2 tablespoons / 25 mL warm water
¼ teaspoon / 1 mL garam masala
Salt to taste
1 dozen small live Maryland blue crabs,
   steamed and shells cracked slightly
   (see Tips)
1 cup / 250 mL water

IN a blender, grind together the dried red chiles, cumin seeds, mustard seeds, turmeric, garlic, and ginger. ✳ Heat the oil in a large nonstick skillet over medium heat. Add the onion; sauté until golden brown. Add the spice paste; sauté for another minute. ✳ Stir in the coconut, tamarind paste, garam masala, salt, and crabs; sauté for 3 to 4 minutes. Add the water. Reduce heat to low, cover, and simmer for 5 minutes. Uncover and cook for another few minutes until almost dry. ✳ Serve hot. ✳ VARIATIONS: You can use frozen crabs for this recipe. There is no need to steam the frozen crabs; just sauté them in the spices long enough to cook them through. You can use crab meat, lobster meat, or imitation crab meat in this dish as well.

EACH SERVING PROVIDES: CALORIES: 180; PROTEIN: 7 G; CARBOHYDRATES: 9 G; FAT: 12 G

I owe this mouth-watering recipe to Sister Francisca of the Convent of St. Brigitta's in Bangalore, India. She would serve it to us, the boarders at the convent, on Friday nights when no meat was allowed.

Tips: To steam crabs: Place crabs in a very large pot with a rack and tight-fitting lid. Add 1 cup / 125 mL each of water and vinegar. Steam, covered, until crabs turn bright red (20 to 30 minutes).

Cracking the shells of the crabs before adding to the spices allows the spices to penetrate the meat.

The spice-filled cheesecloth bag (or bouquet garni) in this recipe is called potli in southern India. An authentic potli has 20 or more herbs and spices in it!

Tips: If dried rose petals are not available, use 1 or 2 fresh rose petals. Experiment with adding your favorite herbs and spices to the spice bag.

spice-scented rice
(potli ke chawal)

Prep Time: 5 minutes, plus 30 minutes to soak the rice
Cooking Time: 20 minutes

2 cups / 500 mL basmati rice
3 or 4 bay leaves
2 small cinnamon sticks
1 large black cardamom pod
3 or 4 dry rose petals

¼ teaspoon / 1 mL coriander seeds
4½ cups / 1.125 L water
1 teaspoon / 5 mL vegetable oil
Few drops lemon juice
Salt to taste

SOAK the rice in enough water to cover for 30 minutes. ✳ Tie together in a cheesecloth bag the bay leaves, cinnamon sticks, cardamom pod, rose petals, and coriander seeds. In a saucepan bring the water and the spice bag to a boil. Reduce heat to low and simmer for about 2 minutes. Remove the spice bag. ✳ To the scented water add the drained rice, oil, lemon juice, and salt. Bring to a boil again. Reduce the heat to low and cook, covered, until the rice is done (about 15 minutes). ✳ VARIATIONS: Sauté any leftovers with a cup / 250 mL of cooked ground beef the next day for a flavorful main dish.
EACH SERVING PROVIDES: CALORIES: 390; PROTEIN: 7 G; CARBOHYDRATES: 86 G; FAT: 2 G

These pancakes make wonderful tea-time snacks. They also keep well in the refrigerator for up to 4 days.

Tips: Chickpea flour is used extensively in Indian cooking and is available from most Indian grocery stores. If you have any leftover vegetables, cut them into bite-sized pieces, dip them in a batter of chickpea flour and water, and panfry them for a delicious Indian tempura!

chickpea pancakes**

Prep Time: 10 minutes
Cooking Time: 10 minutes

1 cup / 250 mL chickpea flour
1½ cups / 375 mL (approx.) water
1 small onion, chopped
1 green chile, chopped

½ teaspoon / 2 mL turmeric
¼ teaspoon / 1 mL red chile powder
4 teaspoons / 20 mL vegetable oil

IN a bowl stir together the flour and the water to form a batter of pouring consistency, much like a pancake batter. Add the onion, green chile, turmeric, and chile powder. Mix well. ✳ Heat a small nonstick skillet over medium heat. Pour a generous ¼ cup / 60 mL of the batter into the skillet. Pour 1 teaspoon / 5 mL of the oil along the edges of the pancake. Cook for about a minute, until bubbles appear on the surface. Flip the pancake over and cook for another 1 to 2 minutes until the underside is firm and no liquid remains. Drain the pancake on paper towels and keep warm covered with a paper towel. Repeat with the remaining batter to make 4 pancakes. ✳ Serve warm. ✳ VARIATIONS: Add 1 tablespoon / 15 mL of finely chopped fresh coriander to the batter.
EACH SERVING PROVIDES: CALORIES: 240; PROTEIN: 12 G; CARBOHYDRATES: 34 G; FAT: 4 G

vermicelli in sweet cream sauce (seviyan)

Prep Time: 5 minutes
Cooking Time: 30 minutes

• •

2 tablespoons / 25 mL butter

½ cup / 125 mL vermicelli, broken

2 cups / 500 mL 1% milk

2 tablespoons / 25 mL low-fat sweetened
  condensed milk

1 teaspoon / 5 mL ground cardamom

Garnish: Golden raisins, slivered almonds,
  and silver foil (varak)

MELT the butter in a small nonstick skillet over medium-high heat. Add the vermicelli. Fry, stirring frequently, until the vermicelli is golden brown. Set aside. ❋ In a large, heavy saucepan, bring the 1% milk to a boil. Add the condensed milk, cardamom, and vermicelli. ❋ Reduce heat to medium-low and cook, stirring constantly, until the milk reduces by half (about 15 minutes). ❋ Serve hot or cold. Garnish with raisins, almonds, and silver foil. ❋ VARIATIONS: You can use any thin spaghetti for this recipe. Add a pinch of saffron for a richer taste.

EACH SERVING PROVIDES: CALORIES: 187; PROTEIN: 5 G; CARBOHYDRATES: 20 G; FAT: 8 G

yogurt rice

• •

MOUND any leftover spice-scented rice on a serving plate. Make a wide, shallow well in the center. (The following amounts are for about 1 cup / 250 mL rice; adjust as necessary for the amount of rice you have.) Add 1 tablespoon / 15 mL each of plain yogurt and milk to the well. Let sit, covered, overnight. ❋ Heat 1 teaspoon / 5 mL oil in a nonstick skillet over medium heat. Add 2 or 3 curry leaves, 1 dried chile pepper, and ¼ teaspoon / 1 mL mustard seeds. When the mustard seeds being to crackle, remove from the heat and pour over the rice. Serve.

This dish is believed to have originated in the palaces of the Mogul emperors of India in the 1500s. This popular dish is traditionally served during the Islamic holy time of Eid. (Vermicelli, by the way, are long rice noodles.)

Tips: For festive occasions, garnish with edible flowers.

THIS MENU IS FOR THE BRAVE AT HEART — OR STOMACH! But don't let spiciness scare you away. You can still enjoy these recipes. If you are a little chile shy, just reduce the amount of chiles. ※ These dishes may be hot but they're still very flavorful. The delicious Indian flavors are not overwhelmed by the spiciness.

· · · · · · · · · ·

Serves 4
——※——

some like it hot

◈ = EXPRESS MENU

Many people use the black seeds of the papaya in salads. Papaya is known to aid digestion.

papaya passion

Prep Time: 2 minutes
Cooking Time: None

2 cups / 500 mL peeled and cubed
   fresh papaya
2 cups / 500 mL water
1 tablespoon / 15 mL light (5%) cream

10 fresh mint leaves
Sugar to taste
5 ice cubes

IN a blender combine the papaya, water, cream, mint, sugar, and ice. Blend until smooth. Serve immediately. ✳ VARIATIONS: Add about 1 teaspoon / 5 mL of grated fresh coconut to the drink for a more exotic flavor.

EACH SERVING PROVIDES: CALORIES: 57; PROTEIN: 1 G; CARBOHYDRATES: 13 G; FAT: 1 G

WEB BITES | eHow provides some helpful tips on picking out ripe papayas: http://www.ehow.com/eHow/eHow/0,1053,3079,FF.html

The contrast between the sweetness of the corn and the heat of the chiles gives this recipe a remarkable taste.

Tips: Rock salt is a staple of Ayurvedic medicine. This black or dark purple salt is actually pink when crushed. Don't be put off by its pungent odor. Try it, and you will soon swear by it too!

chile corn***

Prep Time: 5 minutes
Cooking Time: None

1 small onion, chopped
4 green chiles, chopped
1 small tomato, chopped
2 cups / 500 mL cooked corn kernels
2 tablespoons / 25 mL lemon juice
1 tablespoon / 15 mL chopped
   fresh coriander

1 teaspoon / 5 mL chaat masala
1 teaspoon / 5 mL rock salt
Pinch of red chile powder
Garnish: Lemon wedges

IN a bowl combine the onion, chiles, tomato, corn, lemon juice, coriander, chaat masala, salt, and chile powder; mix well. Chill. Serve garnished with lemon wedges. ✳ VARIATIONS: Try this salad with a cup / 250 mL of cooked chickpeas.

EACH SERVING PROVIDES: CALORIES: 81; PROTEIN: 2 G; CARBOHYDRATES: 19 G; FAT: TRACE

WEB BITES | Here is an article about different types of salt used in cooking: http://detnews.com/2000/food/0817/salt/salt.htm

yogurt and red chile curry***

Prep Time: 5 minutes
Cooking Time: 30 minutes

. . . .

1 tablespoon / 15 mL vegetable oil	1 tablespoon / 15 mL ginger garlic paste
1 teaspoon / 5 mL mustard seeds	2 cups / 500 mL fat-free plain yogurt
¼ teaspoon / 1 mL fenugreek seeds	2 cups / 500 mL water
1 small onion, chopped	¼ teaspoon / 1 mL turmeric
3 whole red chiles	Salt to taste
Leaves from 2 sprigs curry	

HEAT the oil in a medium nonstick skillet over medium heat. Add the mustard seeds and fenugreek seeds. When the mustard seeds begin to crackle, add the onion, red chiles, curry leaves, and ginger garlic paste; sauté until the onion is golden brown (about 2 minutes). Remove from the heat. ✳ In a large saucepan, whisk the yogurt and the water until well blended. Add the cooked onion mixture, turmeric, and salt. Mix well. Bring to a boil over medium heat. Reduce heat to low and simmer for 3 to 4 minutes, stirring constantly. ✳ Serve warm. ✳ VARIATIONS: If you can tolerate the heat, garnish with a few chopped green chiles.

EACH SERVING PROVIDES: CALORIES: 148; PROTEIN: 7 G; CARBOHYDRATES: 15 G; FAT: 4 G

Don't be fooled by the white color of this curry. The red chile gives it a stunning taste and a kick to match.

Tips: Serve this curry with steamed white rice for a wonderfully spicy meal.

chicken 65***

Prep Time: 15 minutes
Cooking Time: 20 minutes

. . . .

1 cup / 250 mL fat-free plain yogurt	1 teaspoon / 5 mL red chile powder
1 cup / 250 mL water	Salt to taste
1 pound / 500 g skinless, boneless chicken breasts, cubed	2 tablespoons / 25 mL finely chopped fresh coriander
¼ teaspoon / 1 mL turmeric	1 teaspoon / 5 mL chaat masala
2 drops red food coloring	1 teaspoon / 5 mL garam masala
2 tablespoons / 25 mL ginger garlic paste	½ teaspoon / 2 mL carom seeds (ajwain)

FOR THE TADKA:

1 tablespoon / 15 mL vegetable oil	¼ teaspoon / 1 mL mustard seeds
1 tablespoon / 15 mL finely chopped fresh mint	3 to 4 green chiles, slit lengthwise
	Leaves from 2 sprigs curry

IN a large saucepan, whisk together the yogurt and water. Stir in the chicken. Bring to a boil over medium heat, stirring occasionally. ✳ Lower the heat. Stir in the turmeric,

CONTINUED . . .

Chicken 65 is a very popular snack at Indian pubs and bars. I am not quite sure where the dish got its name. The original recipe requires that the chicken be deep-fried. I have adapted it to leave out the oil.

Tips: Chicken breast is a very tender meat. Be careful not to overcook it or it will be rubbery.

red food coloring, and ginger garlic paste; cook, stirring, for 2 minutes. Stir in the chile powder and salt. Cook, stirring occasionally, until the liquid starts to dry out. Add the coriander, chaat masala, garam masala, and carom seeds; mix well. Sauté until the liquid completely dries out. Remove from the heat. ✳ In a small nonstick skillet, heat the oil over medium heat. Add the mint, mustard seeds, green chiles, and curry leaves. As soon as the mustard seeds start to crackle, add to the chicken. Mix well. ✳ Serve hot. ✳ VARIATIONS: You can use lamb or beef here as well.

EACH SERVING PROVIDES: CALORIES: 220; PROTEIN: 31 G; CARBOHYDRATES: 11 G; FAT: 5 G

green pea pilaf
(mattar wale chawal)*

Prep Time: 5 minutes, plus 30 minutes for soaking rice
Cooking Time: 20 minutes

2 cups / 500 mL rice, soaked in water
1 tablespoon / 15 mL vegetable oil
1 teaspoon / 5 mL cumin seeds
1 cup / 250 mL green peas

4 cups / 1 L water
Salt to taste
Few drops lemon juice

DRAIN the rice. Heat the oil in a large saucepan over medium heat. Add the cumin seeds and rice; sauté for 1 minute. Add the peas. Sauté for another minute. Add the water, salt, and lemon juice. Bring to a boil. Lower the heat and cook, covered, until the rice is tender (about 15 minutes). ✳ VARIATIONS: Add your choice of cooked vegetables instead of the peas.

EACH SERVING PROVIDES: CALORIES: 370; PROTEIN: 11 G; CARBOHYDRATES: 96 G; FAT: 4 G

WEB BITES | Indian basmati rice has a long history. Read all about it at: http://www.tilda.com

ginger pickle

Prep Time: 10 minutes, plus 48 hours for marinating
Cooking Time: None

1 cup / 250 mL julienned ginger

1 cup / 250 mL lemon juice

PUT the ginger and lemon juice in a jar. Close the lid and shake gently to mix well. Keep in a cool place. The pickle is ready when the ginger has turned pink (about 48 hours). ✳ VARIATIONS: Add a few slit green chiles for a spicy variation. ✳ YIELD: 1 cup / 250 mL. Serving size is 2 tablespoons / 25 mL.

EACH SERVING PROVIDES: CALORIES: 26; PROTEIN: 1 G; CARBOHYDRATES: 5 G; FAT: TRACE

Pilafs were introduced into Indian cooking by the Persian Mogul emperors of the 1500s. The Indian word for pilaf, "pullao," comes from the Persian word "polo," for rice. Pilaf can be served as a side dish to virtually any curry or as an entrée.

This dish is very similar to Japanese gari, the ginger pickle that is served with sushi.

Tips: This pickle keeps in the fridge for 3 to 4 days.

apricots and cream
(khubani meetha)

Prep Time: 5 minutes, plus soaking overnight
Cooking Time: 20 minutes

1 pound / 500 g dried apricots

Garnish: Light (5%) cream

3 tablespoons / 45 mL sugar

PUT the apricots and 2 tablespoons / 25 mL of the sugar in a medium saucepan. Add enough water to just cover the apricots. Stir to dissolve the sugar. Let soak overnight. ❋ Stir in the remaining 1 tablespoon / 15 mL sugar. Bring to a boil. Boil until the apricots are tender (10 to 12 minutes). Use a potato masher to mash the apricots until smooth. Return to the heat and simmer, stirring occasionally, until the apricots are a thick custard-like consistency. ❋ Serve garnished with spoonfuls of cream. ❋ VARIATIONS: If you like, garnish with slivered almonds or silver foil. ❋ YIELD: 4 servings, with leftovers

EACH SERVING PROVIDES: CALORIES: 80; PROTEIN: TRACE; CARBOHYDRATES: 18 G; FAT: TRACE

tomato rice

IF you have any leftover pilaf, sauté it with ½ cup / 125 mL of finely chopped tomato and 2 or 3 whole dried red chiles for a flaming rice entrée.

In North India, apricots are called khubani and are often used in specialty chicken dishes. You can also serve this dish with vanilla ice cream instead of fresh cream.

Tips: If you like a smoother consistency, press the mashed apricots through a sieve.

Serves 4
— ☀ —

HERE IS OUR DAILY BREAD. I added this section after a friend, who was looking over the other recipes, casually asked, "This is great, but what do you eat on a Monday night?" ☀ I will frequently marinate meat and freeze it, so when I get home from work, all I have to do is defrost it and stick it in the oven. ☀ This *is* my express menu.

• • • • • • • • • •

☀ our daily bread

Tea is grown in more than 3,000 tea gardens in India. Making the perfect cup of tea is an art, not a science, so experiment until you get it just right for you. My husband and my friend Mani make the most perfect cup of tea I've ever had.

Tips: This tea is legendary for its digestive powers. Don't store tea leaves in the refrigerator.

Here is a different use for turnips, which are generally used in stews. I savored these patties at a small hotel on the outskirts of New Delhi. They really do melt in your mouth.

indian spice tea (chai)

Prep Time: 2 minutes
Cooking Time: 10 minutes

4 cups / 1 L water
4 bags black tea
¼ teaspoon / 1 mL grated ginger

Milk to taste
Sugar to taste

IN a large saucepan, bring the water to a boil. Add the tea bags and ginger. Reduce heat and simmer for 2 minutes. Add milk to taste. Return to a boil. Remove from the heat and remove tea bags. Add sugar to taste. ❋ Serve hot. ❋ VARIATIONS: One popular variation is to use 1 teaspoon / 5 mL of ground cardamom instead of the grated ginger. EACH SERVING PROVIDES: CALORIES: 52; PROTEIN: 1 G; CARBOHYDRATES: 12 G; FAT: TRACE

WEB BITES | I thoroughly enjoyed this book on Indian tea:
http://www.chai-land.com/chaibook.shtml

turnip treats (shalgam kebabs)*

Prep Time: 10 minutes
Cooking Time: 45 minutes

2 large turnips, peeled and quartered
2 large potatoes, peeled and quartered
1 tablespoon / 15 mL chickpea flour
1 tablespoon / 15 mL French's Fried Onions, pounded

1 tablespoon / 15 mL finely chopped fresh coriander
1 teaspoon / 5 mL salt
½ teaspoon / 2 mL red chile powder
½ teaspoon / 2 mL garam masala

IN a large pot of lightly salted water, boil the turnips and potatoes until tender. Drain the vegetables. Mash the turnips and potatoes. Add the chickpea flour, onions, coriander, salt, chile powder, and garam masala; knead the mixture. ❋ Divide into 8 balls. Flatten each ball in the palms of your hands to make patties about 1 inch / 2.5 cm in diameter and ¼ inch / 5 mm thick. ❋ Heat a large skillet over medium heat. Spray with vegetable cooking spray. Fry the patties in batches until golden brown on each side (about 2 minutes per side), carefully turning them once (the patties are fragile). ❋ VARIATIONS: If you are not a fan of turnips, use grated paneer instead. EACH SERVING PROVIDES (2 PATTIES PER SERVING): CALORIES: 59; PROTEIN: 2 G; CARBOHYDRATES: 9 G; FAT: TRACE

WEB BITES | The Homearts Web site did a special on turnips, with some interesting recipes:
http://food.homearts.com/food/cookings/calen/17cala46.htm

chicken in fenugreek sauce
(methi chicken)*

Prep Time: 15 minutes
Cooking Time: 45 minutes

1 tablespoon / 15 mL vegetable oil

2 onions, chopped

2 large tomatoes, chopped

1 green chile, slit lengthwise

1 tablespoon / 15 mL ginger garlic paste

2 tablespoons / 25 mL finely chopped
   fresh coriander

2 tablespoons / 25 mL finely chopped
   dried fenugreek leaves

1 teaspoon / 5 mL turmeric

1 teaspoon / 5 mL red chile powder

¼ teaspoon / 1 mL garam masala

Salt to taste

8 chicken drumsticks, skinned

1 cup / 250 mL water

2 tablespoons / 25 mL fat-free sour cream

HEAT the oil in a large nonstick skillet over medium heat. Add the onions; sauté until golden. Add the tomatoes, green chile, and ginger garlic paste. Sauté for 3 to 4 minutes or until the tomatoes are soft. If necessary, add 2 tablespoons / 25 mL of water to keep the mixture from sticking. Cook, stirring occasionally, until all the liquid dries up. The masala, as this mixture is called, is done when the oil bubbles on the sides of the mixture. ✻ Turn the heat down to medium-low. Add the coriander, fenugreek, turmeric, chile powder, garam masala, and salt. Sauté for another minute. ✻ Add the chicken. Increase heat to medium and sauté for 3 to 4 minutes, turning the chicken frequently until it is browned all over. Add the water. Cover and cook until the chicken is cooked through (about 25 minutes). ✻ Remove from the heat. Stir in the sour cream. Serve hot. ✻ VARIATIONS: I have used paneer in place of the chicken. Cook for about 10 minutes after the tomato mixture has cooked — long enough to heat the paneer.

EACH SERVING PROVIDES: CALORIES: 240; PROTEIN: 26 G; CARBOHYDRATES: 16 G; FAT: 9 G

This simple chicken curry is my husband's favorite dish. The fenugreek gives it a sensational aroma and a unique taste.

Tips: Some people like to soak the dried fenugreek leaves in hot water for about 10 minutes to soften them before using.

A staple in North Indian homes, rotis are served with most meals. Years ago when I first started making rotis, my father (and later even my husband) would always tease me that eating my rotis was also a geography lesson — each one was shaped like some continent! It took me a long time to get them to be round, but I am not ashamed to admit that even today sometimes one comes out looking like South America.

Tips: To ensure that the skillet is warm enough, sprinkle it with some dry flour. If it quickly turns reddish brown, the skillet is ready.

Rotis freeze well for about 2 weeks. To reheat, sprinkle a few drops of water on each roti, cover with a paper towel, and microwave for a few seconds.

our daily bread: roti

Prep Time: 20 minutes
Cooking Time: 20 minutes

2 cups / 500 mL whole wheat flour   ¾ cup / 175 mL water
Pinch of salt

In a mixing bowl stir together the flour and salt. Add the water and knead until the dough is flexible and no longer sticky (about 5 minutes). Set aside for about 15 minutes. ❋ Divide the dough into 8 portions. Roll each portion into a ball and roll it in a little flour. Flatten it between the palms of your hands. On a lightly floured surface, roll into thin 8-inch / 20-cm rounds. ❋ Heat a small nonstick skillet over medium heat. Cook 1 round at a time for 30 seconds. Flip over and cook for another 30 seconds. With a small folded cloth, press down lightly on the round. The roti will start to puff up. Don't worry if it does not — it takes a lot of practice to get this to work right! Place the roti on a serving plate lined with paper towels. Keep warm, covered with a paper towel. Repeat for the remaining rotis. ❋ Serve immediately, or wrap in foil and reheat in a 300°F / 150°C oven until warmed through. ❋ Variations: Add a pinch of red chile powder and rock salt to the dough to make a chile roti. Serve with any yogurt sauce or raita. ❋ Makes: 8 rotis

Each Serving Provides: Calories: 217; Protein: 7 g; Carbohydrates: 46 g; Fat: 1 g

sliced onion salad (pyaz ka salad)*

Prep Time: 5 minutes
Cooking Time: None

1 large red onion, thinly sliced
3 green chiles, slit lengthwise
Chaat masala to taste
Lemon juice to taste

ARRANGE the onion and green chiles on a serving plate. Sprinkle with the chaat masala and lemon juice. Serve. ⁂ VARIATIONS: Add sliced cucumber and sliced tomatoes for different texture and color.

EACH SERVING PROVIDES: CALORIES: 16; PROTEIN: TRACE; CARBOHYDRATES: 3 G; FAT: TRACE

Nothing is simpler to make or more delicious to eat than this sliced onion salad. That is just my humble opinion.

Tips: If the onion tastes too tart, soak it in cold water for about 20 minutes. Drain and then use.

carrot pudding (gajjar ka halwa)

Prep Time: 15 minutes
Cooking Time: 45 minutes

2 cups / 500 mL 1% milk
1 cup / 250 mL coarsely grated peeled carrots
Pinch of saffron, soaked in 2 tablespoons / 25 mL warm milk
2 tablespoons / 25 mL sugar
Garnish: Slivered blanched almonds

IN a large, heavy saucepan, bring the milk and the carrots to a boil. Reduce heat to medium-low and simmer, stirring occasionally, until the milk has reduced by half (about 35 minutes). ⁂ Stir in the saffron and sugar. Simmer, stirring occasionally, for another 15 to 20 minutes or until the carrots have cooked completely. The pudding should be thick. ⁂ Serve warm, garnished with slivered almonds. ⁂ VARIATIONS: Instead of almonds, you can garnish with a sprinkle of cinnamon.

EACH SERVING PROVIDES: CALORIES: 160; PROTEIN: 6 G; CARBOHYDRATES: 17 G; FAT: 7 G

My mother makes this dessert all the time. I am still trying to figure out what her secret ingredient is, because mine never tastes the same! Maybe it is 30 years of practice.

fenugreek curry bread

· ·

PUT any remaining curry sauce from the Chicken in Fenugreek Sauce in a mixing bowl; add enough water to make a paste. Knead in enough whole wheat flour to make a dough. Divide the dough into golf-ball-sized balls. On a lightly floured surface, roll out each ball into a thin 5-inch / 12-cm circle. Dry roast in a small skillet over medium heat until browned on each side.

chicken frankie

· ·

IF you have any chicken pieces and roti left over, shred the chicken, roll up in the roti (like a burrito), and serve warm.

Serves 4
— ✻ —

PRESIDENT BILL CLINTON AND HIS DAUGHTER, CHELSEA, visited India in March 2000, making him the first American president after nearly 21 years to visit the Subcontinent. Clinton stayed at the Maurya Sheraton in New Delhi. He and Chelsea enjoyed several meals at the hotel's premier Mogul restaurant, Bukhara. The staff at the Bukhara Restaurant, charmed by Bill and Chelsea, named a platter after him and another after Chelsea. ✻ I was in India at the time, and the food detective that I am, I decided to see what the president had eaten. Instead, I ended up ordering the Chelsea Platter. I present to you my versions of the dishes in the Chelsea Platter. There is no way I can replicate the awesome cooking of the chefs at Bukhara, one of India's best restaurants, but my dad, my mom, and I tried and tried until the recipes tasted about the same! ✻ There is no express version of this menu, nor are there any drinks or appetizers, since it was a platter with a number of choices. I would suggest Indian Flat Bread on the side. For dessert, Chelsea enjoyed the No-Cook Indian Ice Cream. Mine is a poor man's version of the rich whole-milk kulfi served at Bukhara.

. . . .

the chelsea platter

✻

where's the real food?

on the side

live a little

Indian cheese, or paneer, is very versatile. You can fry it, bake it, or scramble it, and it always tastes wonderful. (Yes, I did try to boil it once. My advice is, DON'T.)

Tips: To prevent the cheese cubes from melting or charring, watch the dish closely. Depending on the size of the cubes, a few minutes in the oven may be enough.

tandoori indian cheese cubes (tandoori paneer)*

Prep Time: 15 minutes
Cooking Time: 45 minutes

1 egg
2 tablespoons / 25 mL low-fat sour cream
½ teaspoon / 2 mL turmeric
½ teaspoon / 2 mL red chile powder

½ teaspoon / 2 mL garam masala
Salt to taste
1 cup / 250 mL cubed paneer
　(1-inch / 2.5-cm cubes)

IN a medium bowl, beat the egg. Add the sour cream, turmeric, chile powder, garam masala, and salt. Stir together well. Add the paneer cubes, stirring to coat. Refrigerate for about 20 minutes. ✳ Meanwhile, preheat the oven to 300°F / 150°C. ✳ Place the cheese cubes in a baking dish. Bake for 10 minutes or until golden brown. ✳ Serve hot. ✳ VARIATIONS: Chicken cubes can be substituted for the cheese cubes. Increase the cooking time so the chicken cooks completely.
EACH SERVING PROVIDES: CALORIES: 146; PROTEIN: 12 G; CARBOHYDRATES: 4 G; FAT: 6 G

The Bukhara's version, though outstanding in taste, was deep-fried and had a lot of nuts. I have tried my hand at a healthier version here.

Tips: It's faster to bake potatoes in the microwave. Prick them first to let the steam escape.

spicy potato cups (tandoori aloo)**

Prep Time: 15 minutes
Cooking Time: 45 minutes

2 large potatoes, baked
1 teaspoon / 5 mL vegetable oil
1 green chile, finely chopped
2 tablespoons / 25 mL finely chopped onion
1 tablespoon / 15 mL grated paneer
2 tablespoons / 25 mL finely chopped
　fresh coriander

½ teaspoon / 2 mL red chile powder
½ teaspoon / 2 mL mango powder
Salt to taste
Garnish: Pinch of chaat masala

REMOVE the skin of the potatoes and cut the potatoes in half. Create a potato cup by scooping out the center, leaving a wall ¼ inch / 5 mm thick. Set aside the potato cups and insides. ✳ Heat the oil in a nonstick skillet over medium heat. Add the green chile, onion, and paneer; sauté for 2 minutes. Add the scooped-out potato, coriander, chile powder, mango powder, and salt. Sauté for another 2 minutes. Let cool. ✳ Spoon the mixture equally into each of the potato cups. Sprinkle with chaat masala and serve at room temperature. ✳ VARIATIONS: You can create bowls with your choice of vegetable. Tomato bowls taste particularly good.
EACH SERVING PROVIDES: CALORIES: 100; PROTEIN: 2 G; CARBOHYDRATES: 19 G; FAT: 2 G

peppered cauliflower florets
(mazedar gobi)

Prep Time: 10 minutes
Cooking Time: 10 minutes

. . . .

2 cups / 500 mL vegetable oil   1 teaspoon / 5 mL chaat masala
1 cup / 250 mL cauliflower florets

HEAT the oil in a wok over medium-high heat. Fry the cauliflower in batches until golden brown. Drain on paper towels. ❋ Sprinkle with the chaat masala and serve immediately. ❋ VARIATIONS: Use any vegetable of your choice. (Try potatoes, broccoli, or sweet potatoes.)

EACH SERVING PROVIDES: CALORIES: 135; PROTEIN: 2 G; CARBOHYDRATES: 3 G; FAT: 12 G

The hotel's recipe was deep-fried in a gram flour batter. I do not like the heaviness the batter adds, so my version is without the batter. Try both and see which you prefer.

Tips: Ensure that the cauliflower florets are completely dry before you fry them. This will prevent the oil from splattering.

mother of all lentils
(maa ki dal)*

Prep Time: 15 minutes, plus soaking overnight
Cooking Time: 2 hours

. . . .

1½ cups / 375 mL black lentils   1 teaspoon / 5 mL red chile powder
6 cups / 1.5 L water   Salt to taste
2 small tomatoes, peeled   ¼ cup / 60 mL light (5%) cream
2 tablespoons / 25 mL butter   Garnish: Chopped fresh coriander
1 tablespoon / 15 mL ginger garlic paste

SOAK the lentils overnight. Drain the lentils and put them in a large, heavy saucepan. Add the water and bring to a boil. Lower the heat and simmer, uncovered, for 1 hour. The lentils will start to split. ❋ Using a potato masher, coarsely mash the lentils with the cooking water. Add the tomatoes, butter, ginger garlic paste, chile powder, and salt. Simmer, stirring occasionally, for another hour or until the lentils are creamy and completely cooked. ❋ Stir in the cream; simmer for 10 minutes. Serve warm, garnished with coriander. ❋ VARIATIONS: These lentils can be cooked overnight in a slow cooker. Increase the water to 8½ cups / 2.125 L. Cooking time will be about 12 hours.

EACH SERVING PROVIDES: CALORIES: 220; PROTEIN: 13 G; CARBOHYDRATES: 33 G; FAT: 5 G

This spectacular delicacy is one of the most popular dals, or lentils, in North India. Traditionally it is cooked for more than 8 hours in a slow cooker. Serve it with rice, rotis, or naans.

Tips: Prepare this the day ahead; it tastes better once the flavors have had a chance to meld.

colored bell peppers with cheese filling (paneer wali simla mirch)*

Prep Time: 30 minutes
Cooking Time: 30 minutes

When I first started making these, I would stuff whole bell peppers. However, I noticed that most of my guests would eat only half a pepper, so I modified the recipe to use half bell peppers.

6 medium bell peppers (different colors)
1 tablespoon / 15 mL vegetable oil
1 small onion, finely chopped
1 green chile, chopped
1-inch / 2.5-cm piece peeled
   ginger, julienned
1 teaspoon / 5 mL cumin seeds
1 tomato, finely chopped

2 tablespoons / 25 mL finely chopped
   fresh coriander
2 cups / 500 mL grated paneer
½ teaspoon / 2 mL turmeric
½ teaspoon / 2 mL red chile powder
¼ cup / 60 mL light (5%) cream
Salt to taste
Garnish: Grilled red bell pepper strips

FINELY dice 1 red and 1 green bell pepper. Set aside. ✳ Preheat the oven to 300°F / 150°C. ✳ Slice of the top of the remaining 4 peppers. Remove the seeds. Place peppers cut side down in a roasting pan and spray with vegetable cooking spray. Roast until brown spots start to appear on the skins (about 5 minutes). ✳ Remove the peppers from the oven; do not turn off the oven. Put the peppers in a paper bag; seal and let stand for 10 minutes. (The steam inside the bag will help to loosen the skins.) When the peppers are cool enough to handle, peel them. Set aside. ✳ In a nonstick skillet over medium heat, heat the oil. Add the onion, green chile, ginger, and cumin seeds; sauté for 2 minutes. Add all the reserved diced peppers, tomato, and coriander. Sauté for 2 to 3 minutes. Add the paneer; sauté for 1 minute. Add the turmeric and chile powder; sauté for another minute. Stir in the cream and salt. Remove from the heat. ✳ Stuff each pepper with the filling. Place the peppers on a baking sheet and bake for 5 minutes or until heated through. ✳ Serve with grilled red peppers on the side. ✳ VARIATIONS: Add your choice of filling to this recipe. Minced cooked chicken or leftover rice pilaf work well. ✳ YIELD: 4 servings, with leftovers

EACH SERVING PROVIDES: CALORIES: 320; PROTEIN: 18 G; CARBOHYDRATES: 17 G; FAT: 8 G

WEB BITES | This article has pictures showing the best way to roast bell peppers: http://living.yahoo.com/living/features/ci/ 20001024_the_best_way_to_roast_bell_peppers_m.html

a final word

. . . .

JUST as I was getting ready to wrap up the manuscript for this book, my husband was peeking over my shoulder and asked, "So what did President Clinton eat?" So for all you curious people out there, here is what was on the Clinton Platter:

Sikandari raan: leg of lamb cooked with dark spices

Murg tandoori: tandoori chicken

Barrah kabob: lamb kebabs

Murg malai: chicken with heavy cream

Shish kabob: lamb kebabs

Dal Bukhara: maa ki dal (mother of all lentils)

Assorted raita

Kulfi: Indian ice cream

INTERNET

EthnicGrocer.com: www.ethnicgrocer.com

IndianGroceryNet.com: www.indiangrocerynet.com (This interesting site will send you premeasured ingredients based on recipes you select.)

Indian Grocery Shops List: members.theglobe.com/jsukumar (This site provides a detailed list of about 200 Indian mail order and/or local grocery stores in about 15 countries.)

IndiaPlaza.com: www.indiaplaza.com

Kundan Foods.com: www.kundanfoods.com

Namaste.com: www.namaste.com

Spices Galore: www.spicesgalore1.com

Spices Store: www.spices-store.com

MAIL ORDER / LOCAL INDIAN GROCERS (UNITED STATES)

House of Spices
127-40 Willets Point Blvd.
Flushing, New York 11368-1506
Tel: (718) 507-4600
E-mail : hosindia@aol.com

India Foods & Spices
80 River Street
Cambridge, Massachusetts 02139-3805
Tel: (617) 497-6144

Spice Corner
135 Lexington Avenue
New York, New York 10016
Tel: (212) 689-5182

The British Express
2880 SW 42nd Avenue
Palm City, Florida 34990
Tel: (888) 840-1280 or (561) 219-0664
Fax: (561) 219-1340

CONTINUED . . .

shopping sources

Mail Order / Local Indian Grocers (Canada)

Annapurna Mithai Shoppe
1544 Warden Avenue
Scarborough, Ontario M1R 2S8
Tel: (416) 449-0157

Dino's Grocery Mart
460 Notre Dame Avenue
Winnipeg, Manitoba R3V 1R5
Tel: (204) 942-1526

Golden Groceries Ltd
7180 Airport Road
Malton, Ontario L4T 2H2
Tel: (905) 612-8288

IndianLife Food Corporation
3835 2nd Avenue
Burnaby, British Columbia V5C 3W7
Tel: (604) 205-9176
Fax: (604) 205-9172
Website: www.indianlife.com

Mississauga Continental Groceries
59 Dundas Street West
Mississauga, Ontario L5B 1H7
Tel: (905) 949-5199

Mail Order / Local Indian Grocers (International)

Comptoir des Indes
67, Bd. de Strasbourg
31000 TOULOUSE France
Tel: 61 22 77 03

Shah-Jahan Grocers
283 High Street North
London East, UK
Tel: 0181 552 4136

Shakti Foods
12/13 Queens Market
London East, UK
Tel: 0181 471 4440

Sohal Food Store
67 Rupert Street
Chesterfield, Derbyshire UK
Tel: 01246 851411

Page numbers in bold indicate references to web sites.

index

about the author

. . . .

A NEW YOUNG VOICE IN INDIAN COOKING, Monica Bhide was probably born with a mixing spoon in her mouth! Since the age of ten, cooking has been a lifelong passion for this accomplished caterer and home chef. Monica specializes in Indian cuisine and has prepared everything from an intimate dinner for two to large parties of 40. A graduate of several formal cooking courses in her native India, she is also a voracious cookbook reader and counts hundreds of cookbooks in her collection.

Frustrated by the lack of straightforward Indian cookbooks, Monica became inspired several years ago to develop simplified and healthful versions of her favorite Indian dishes. The result is this collection of mouthwatering Indian recipes, where Monica, in her down-to-earth and lively writing style, guides Indian food lovers on a non-intimidating and flavorful foray into home-style Indian cooking.

Born in India, thirty-two-year-old Monica grew up in the Middle East, and then moved to the United States in 1991. She has an engineering degree from Bangalore University and two master's in information systems technology from George Washington University. Monica currently resides in Boston with her husband, Sameer, and two-year-old son, Jai.